# 1-Woman
# 1-Motorbike
# 1-Year

## A Guinness World Record Journey

Danell Lynn, M.Ed.

ISBN-13: 978-1545361924

ISBN-10: 1545361924

Mary Ann, Cheers to kicking Cancer's Ass and breaking the confidence Malady the roll will for come. 2017 MAWWR.

# DEDICATION

To all those that said it could not be done…Thank You.

# CONTENTS

# ACKNOWLEDGMENTS

I have a large thank you to the hidden team behind this solo journey -Thank you mom and dad for taking the late night calls, helping to map me out of storms and for believing in this wild journey of mine-even miles away.

Anyone who knows me knows I am an eater – I love my food, thus a large thank you to my grandmother for taking the time to learn new dehydrated meals that kept me fed very well for a year on the road.

To my family that came out at my going away to wish me well and came back for my welcome home! Thank you!

To all those who opened their doors – there are many of you that were a part of this journey, the moto-shops that supported me and the camp grounds that gave us a site. Thank you to all those that provided meals, encouragement, and thank you to the readers that kept this blog alive that is now being turned into a book!

Thank you to my gear and parts sponsors for outfitting this journey (REV'IT, GiantLoop, LoneRider, Triumph, Sena, British Customs, AVON). And the financial books I have devoured for years that helped me realize that in 2 years I could save for a yearlong sabbatical.

# A NOTE

This is a collection of blogs written by the author Danell Lynn during her year long journey to all 50 States and Canada that broke a Guinness World Record. Some blogs have not been included in this book due to length, sequence, or relevance - all writings are as factual as the memory occurred at the time.

For more you can view www.DanellLynn.com

# Driving Force

*Posted on March 21, 2014*

### 1 Woman...1 Bike...1 Year...all 50 US states and Canada...

It is my pleasure to meet you. It is my hope that in reading or following this blog it inspires adventure!

I am the couturier for Dl-Couture fashion house and designer of Humani Handbags...an author, adventurer, philanthropist...and I ride motorcycles...welcome to the journey.

I grew up traveling and moving often and never quite found that place one calls home, I never know how to answer the age-old question, "where are you from?" I tend to say "everywhere" as for me the current place that feels the most like home is the open road. Will this journey change that for me? It is possible, I also wonder as I take on all 50 states of my birth country, will I find a state that will let my roots grow? Only time will tell.

What is the driving force behind wanting to spend a year on the road, camping and motorbiking?

For me it comes with an accent all its own, a rumble that excites, the non-conformity of an outlier, daring to breathe in fear and saying yes to adventure...this is my driving force...and I take to it gladly with my knight in shining armor-my Triumph Bonneville!

(This was my very first blog entry and began the thread 6 months pre-departure) – Enjoy the Ride!

# MADV Moto magazine – RIF

*Posted on March 31, 2014 in Press*

We get into a routine and the drag of the daily repetition where something as simple as checking your mailbox becomes another task.

Unless that is - you are anxiously awaiting the new issue of ADV Moto Magazine! Daily I would get out of work, find parking at my complex and briskly walk to #2021 for a mail check. I would insert the key with excitement, often to reveal a coupon newspaper and a bill. Oh but last night was different, there it sat beautifully wrapped in plastic, the new ADV Moto issue 79!

RIF – Reader In Focus feature and the first printed press on the upcoming adventure for Black tie 2 Black top. It is a great layout and wonderful to be a part of a magazine that I have devoured for years! Thank you to Nicole and Paul for the support.

This is the start of much more press to come, and the monotony of picking up an article or coverage or TV program...that just never does get old!

## April 2014

### Storm before the Calm
*April 30, 2014 // 0 Comments*

Storm before the calm, at 2:30 am I woke with the realization that I would be on the road, full-on adventuring, in less than 4.5 month! My heart was racing and I tossed and [...]

### WHY
*April 29, 2014 // 1 Comment*

BUT WHY... Living is about grabbing life by the Coconuts! We have begun to believe that we must stay and live in the comfort zone of what one "should" do! But [...]

### When to leave for an adventure?
*April 20, 2014 // 0 Comments*

Simply put...when you think of nothing else. It is time to live your adventure when you start quieting the voices of fear, or as some call "voices of reason." The key [...]

### Video-Christmas in April
*April 1, 2014 // 0 Comments*

It is 93 degrees in Phoenix today, I quickly jump in the shower to cool down and see the note on my door that a delivery awaits me in the apartment office. I knew what it [...]

DANELL LYNN

# Video-Christmas in April

*Posted on April 1, 2014*

It is 93 degrees in Phoenix, Arizona today, I quickly jump in the shower to cool down and see the note on my door that a delivery awaits me in the apartment office. I knew what it could be, I had no idea that the 2 things I was expecting would come in such a large box...so I filmed my Christmas in April with a moto adventurers version of Santa in Giant Loop- and they had many surprises in store for me!

You can see this video on my channel: www.youtube.com/DanellLynn of direct https://youtu.be/zF8zRfYiaKE

# When to leave for an adventure?

*Posted on April 20, 2014*

Simply put...when you can think of nothing else.

It is time to live your adventure when you start quieting the voices of fear, or as some call "voices of reason." The key to a journey is knowing that it is for you and not for everyone else. It is the time in your life that you should be selfish and embrace your dreams with the understanding that it is okay!

For me I am not a big believer in regrets, and I find

8

journeys, adventures, even daily choices are answered by my asking...will I regret going? Usually what flashes through my mind is I WILL regret NOT going!

So ask yourself, "Will I regret not _____?" Fill in the blank with your adventure.

A short and sweet to the point post about just getting out and living! Go on be free, let your inner adventurer out!

# WHY

*Posted on April 29, 2014*

## BUT WHY... Living is about grabbing life by the Coconuts!

We have begun to believe that we must stay and live in the comfort zone of what one "should" do! But for me, I feel the most alive outside that zone, it is thrilling and invigorates me to push the boundaries a little more!

**"Some people see things as they are and say why? I dream things that never were and say, why not?"**
-Robert F. Kennedy
(Interpretation of George Bernard Shaw's words in the play *Back to Methuselah*)

Dear WHY,

You are not the first to question "What the Hell are you doing?" My first off the cuff answer is -Why NOT? The above quote has been on one wall or another, visible daily for the last 7 years!

I was lucky to be born into a family that values travel. By the time we moved to England (6th grade) I had been to almost all 50 states and many National Parks. Back stateside as a teen and then off to college in Miami, Florida I took a road trip and checked off the last on my list of 50 – Maine by age 19. But again you may say...but WHY then am I traveling to all 50 states? For one I was a child when I visited them last time, as an adult it will be a different perspective. Also my childhood travels were on four-wheels with windows and doors, this time 2 – wheels, wide open with the landscapes I travel through.

When we moved to Europe it really opened doors to travel as a family and I just have not shaken that out of my genes. By my thirties I had been to over 40 countries and noticed relationships between countries and states. For example the mountains in Chile reminded me of the mountains of Hawaii, and so many other correlations started to pop up as I traveled - thus I decided to take a year adventure throughout my own backyard.

I also know that I will not take this trip and stay exactly the same. Journeys of this kind add layers to who you are. One thing for sure is currently the road feels like home to me, and maybe, just maybe I will find a spot to homestead ... but only time will tell, the road may be my lifetime nature.

There are so many reasons when you sit down to take a trip like this, another component for me as a writer and humanitarian is to share the young readers edition of my book *Philanthropic Wanderlust* with students. (called Purposeful Wanderings). I will be doing readings and providing classroom sets with curriculum guides to schools around the nation. Hoping to provide the stepping stones into philanthropy for future generations.

I also plan to do talks and lectures about motorcycle travel around the nation, with a few already scheduled (*extra note – this GWR journey led to many more talks and Keynotes, and Headliners...and hopefully many more to come).

I have never just done ONE thing, so it make since to continue my nature and do book readings, lectures, traveler stories on the road, documentaries, blogs, video blog, write some more, RIDE even more and expand into the world of motorcycle travelers that have been a big part of who I am for a very long time! Thank you to all that have read this, and I look forward to seeing you on the road...the road of life...adventure is calling loudly...go ahead answer it!

So as I hit the road I raise a glass to all those who may say WHY and I hope that one day you say WHY NOT!

-Danell

# Storm before the Calm

*Posted on April 30, 2014 in News, Press*

Storm before the calm, at 2:30 am I woke with the realization that I would be on the road, full-on adventuring, in less than 4.5 months! My heart was racing, I tossed and turned waking up exhausted wondering what the hell am I doing. I knew that I would still be going-there was no question, but the walking away and career breaking for a year, was I crazy.

I never doubted that I would be leaving. Mind you half of my house is either packed for storage or listed on Craigslist for sale, so where was all this anxiety coming from. I am not quite sure where or why but I know that the storm dissipated when I opened my email and had the attached image from Iain Harper of the *Ted Simon Foundation*. My badge was approved and ready, I was now listed as an official Jupiter's Traveller. My grin was ear to ear and warmed my heart – ravaging any anxiety that was left over from my sleepless night.

I am taking the steps that are right, and are towards adventure, filled with unique and memorable experiences. I am not sure what I will learn on the road but it will be a "road education" that will change my life, I have no doubt about that.

.

## May 2014

### Overland Expo 2014

*May 21, 2014 // 0 Comments*

Encompassed by the winds and dust that are as much of a tradition as the event itself, I met up with wonderful friends that I had not seen in at least 6 months and others [...]

## June 2014

### Test Ride – T-4 months

*June 4, 2014 // 4 Comments*

Trying to plan for a year on the road can be daunting...the stress becomes limited with mini-adventures. In these I am able to test my gear and supplies and find out what [...]

# Overland Expo 2014

*Posted on May 21, 2014 in Prep Reel, Travel*

Encompassed by the winds and dust that are as much of a tradition as the event itself, I met up with wonderful friends that I had not seen in at least 6 months and others over a year,

I learned new tools, and this video is one of the newest creations to come from that excitement. *sadly the video does not work on all computers – but here you go: https://spark.adobe.com/v/3iVQY46xgmd

The above picture is my tent testing with my breakfast and kitchen set up – some stuff worked great, others not so well at all.

# Test Ride – T-4 months

*Posted on June 4, 2014 in Prep Reel*

Trying to plan for a year on the road can be daunting...the stress becomes limited with mini-adventures. In these I am able to test my gear and supplies and find out what works and what does not, and what I need to learn to eliminate user error.

Overland Expo fell at the perfect time. I had received my sponsored luggage from Giant Loop and my tent from Lone Rider and was ready to give it all a test-pack and set-up. I decided that I would try to take all items I would be taking on my big adventure. It is T minus 4 months until the big departure and this was a perfect time to give it all a go. This video is test of the camera equipment and riding!

https://youtu.be/VofrzV0mOkg

DANELL LYNN

## August 2014

### Fear
*August 13, 2014 // 9 Comments*

I have noticed the closer my departure day gets and the more radio shows I do, I am asked, "What is your biggest fear, what are your scared of?" It is not [...]

### FOX 10 News
*August 2, 2014 // 1 Comment*

Is great to have the local support and see that words of adventure – creating the life you dream are getting out there. I was excited before but somehow this FOX [...]

# FOX 10 News

*Posted on August 2, 2014  News, Press*

It is great to have the local support and see that words of adventure – creating the life you dream are getting out there. I was excited before but somehow this FOX news segment really hit home, and I am having a hard time shaking off the urge to ride out of town right now... only 49 days to go!

http://www.myfoxphoenix.com/clip/10432926/one-woman-one-motorcyle-and-50-states

# Fear

*Posted on August 13, 2014 in Travel, Why*

I have noticed the closer my departure day gets and the more radio shows I do, I am asked, "What is your biggest fear, what are your scared of?" It is not that I have no fears, a little scared is a very healthy thing, but what people are looking for...is the "ahh, what if someone breaks into my tent" "what if I am attacked riding solo...." While people may worry of that for me, it is not a fear I carry.

I have been a solo traveler for years, and yes there are times where my heart has raced and I have wondered "what the hell am I doing here?" But I have never been attacked, I have only been pick-pocketed. In the developing world travel I have done-into some remote not so "safe" areas for humanitarian work-the worst thing that happened, was a complete car break-in where they stole everything-even my ink pens...and it happened back in Phoenix while I was in the northern mountains of Ecuador 30 miles from the border of Colombia!

It is not being naive to the darkness within humanity, trust me, from a girl with a psychology degree, having been on an EMT ride-along call to a disturbing child scene and an avid reader of true crime novels since my teen years, I understand that people can be quite horrible. But I don't believe in letting the hatred that is only "possible" freeze you into a comfort zone safety net, when in all actuality you could get hit by a bus crossing the street right by your house. It is easy to go into a downward spiral with all the hate that many people currently carry. But imagine what you are missing if you live your life in a fear based state of mind.

If I did not venture to far-flung places I would never have knitted with a grandmother in her home in Ecuador sharing Papayas. I would never have gotten lost in Shanghai and almost in tears when I found my pride in getting back all on my own to my hostel. I would never have helped deliver turtle eggs on the beach in Mexico at midnight. I would never have enjoyed tea with the king's council in Morocco...there are so many memories and journeys that have created a life for me filled with passion that I would never have had if I let fear rule my decisions to see the world. And solo...well that just helps make the world more open to you, many of my memories would not have occurred if I were in a group, so "solo" no it does not scare me.

But what I do fear, is not going. I am scared of living the "typical" 9 to 5 life because it is what you are "supposed" to do! I fear the monotony of routines to just get the j.o.b. done. I am scared to not live life to the fullest!

Everyone's "life to the fullest" is different, for me, if I ask myself -"will I regret not going?" The answer is always yes, so I always must go! I don't believe in regrets, and I do believe in trusting your gut. If I feel nervous fear (this is the good fear – fight or flight) then I walk away from situations, if I go to camp and the woods and this spot is creeping me out, then I drive on until the next great spot.

Fear is a healthy thing, it is good to be scared to a certain degree. When you let either control your life or decisions that is what should truly be feared because at that point so much of life's beauty becomes lost. So that is a long way to say, yes there is nervous fear and I think a little is good, but no it is not "fear" in the worry for my life. Just a "fear" that would accompany packing your entire life into storage, selling all your furniture and your new home being a tent in the vast expansive wilderness...well shit that is excitement not fear! Smile at your fear, give it a hug, and then punch it in the face and take on the adventure you dream of!

## Day One – Remembering the Departure
*September 30, 2014 // 2 Comments*

There I was getting packed and ready, and as any day one starts out of a great adventure...I ran into technical issues! I had just got a SPOT tracker and was trying to [...]

## Hwy 1
*October 18, 2014 // 1 Comment*

The coast of California, Oregon and Washington are well-known rides, and having been on parts of them before – I found beauty in the ever-changing elements of life. [...]

## Helmet Time
*October 15, 2014 // 4 Comments*

For weeks I have found this trip was not yet my own. I was trying to see all that I could and still make it in time for planned talks, news programs, and visits...all [...]

# Day One –Remembering the Departure

*Posted on September 30, 2014 in Travel,*

There I was getting packed and ready, and as any day one starts out of a great adventure...I ran into technical issues! I had just got a SPOT tracker and was trying to get it online and up and running before departing and it just would not connect to the satellite...I read it again "with the SPOT tracker powered-OFF set outside in view for the satellite" ...I thought that was odd and re-read the directions, yep – powered – OFF. After a good 20 minutes I went to the apartment office for wi-fi and called customer support. I read the woman the paragraph on their site and she said "oh my, it is wrong

– you need to turn it ON." So after an hour and half of working thru the kinks the SPOT tracker was online.

Why does this little guy matter – well I am not traveling with a GPS nor a Smart phone and need the GPS satellite tracks to turn in for the attempt of a Guinness World Record-and although just going from Phoenix to Tucson for my first school visit it was important as 130 miles is a 130 mile to add for the total! And it is fun that family and friends can follow along and check where I might be on a certain day. So only about two and half hours later than planned – I hit the road!

Worried a little about this massive inland hurricane style storm that was supposed to hit Phoenix the day before, I fretted mildly that it might hit Friday morning as I departed...but I only got a little rain and the back road was not flooded so I was able to stick to my plan of avoiding major interstates and staying on scenic routes and by-ways as much as possible! I got into Tucson with not much time and would be getting to the school just an hour before dismissal and I needed a quick gas stop!

THE LONGEST 4 Minute mile in HISTORY...

I got gas slapped back on my helmet and drove away, at the second stoplight I felt as if I forgot something...looking at my hands I had my gloves, my gear...oh shit my backpack...Here I am day 1 and it was about to end my trip completely – my wallet, my computer, my new camera, my spot tracker...I flipped a u-turn and zoomed back. Flying into the gas station and there sat my backpack undisturbed! I exhaled and the woman next to the pump stated, "oh is that yours?" Yes I replied and slapped it on as an attendant walked my way. The woman with a shaky voice, "you can never be to sure it is an unmanned backpack at a gas pump we reported it!" With a smile I jumped on my bike and took-off, thinking to myself-Thank god for American Fear, I could have lost all the technical and plastic for the entire trip...I have since changed up the system!

I made it to the school in one of the many moments I am sure will happen again – I wished I had a flying video camera or video crew, it was unexpected but the 5th grade class of Mr. Green at Bonillas was outside waiting for my arrival. They were inside the schools chain link fence and waving. As I drove by to come in the front entrance they took off and ran along the fence with me, waving and shouting as I entered! What an awesome welcome for the first donation of Purposeful Wanderings classroom set!

We did a reading and a talk of the adventure, the students were wonderfully inquisitive and the boys...well boys will be boys... a few wanted to know only what would happen if I got hit by a truck up on hill and rolled down! It was definitely humorous. This classroom is also going to track my trip and Mr. Green's wife Kristina created a wonderful bulletin board for them to follow on the adventure!

# Helmet Time

Posted on October 15, 2014 in Road Thoughts

For weeks I have found this trip was not yet my own, I was trying to see all that I could and still make it in time for planned talks, news programs, and visits...all were lovely and a blast but I had yet to detach the way I originally thought would happen on a solo adventure such as this....until this week!

As I was leaving Oregon and going into Northern California I started to feel everything on a rawer level. The changing of the leaves seemed more vibrant, the air more crisp and as I contemplated why, I realized for the first time there is nothing – not a specific time to be anywhere, nobody is waiting on – or expecting me...it is just me and my "helmet time."

The next day I started to feel my emotions even deeper
– I rode through the twisty mountain roads just me,
Amelia, nature, and the *Snap Judgement* podcast. I love
this NPR program and back home on Sundays at 5pm I
rewound to 1950's and turned off everything but my
radio program...I sat like an 80 year old grandmother
and knitted or puzzled as I listen to the artfully crafted
program. It was powerful then but now with just my
helmet and the sounds and power of stories and
interviews of 5 podcasts I laughed, and cried silent
tears, and I smiled in the simple joys that I was feeling
by letting myself go!

# Hwy 1

*Posted on October 18, 2014 -Travel*

The coast of California, Oregon and Washington are well-known rides, and having been on parts of them before – I found beauty in the ever-changing elements of life. Part of my first week and into my second was spent on the famous coastal highway 1 and the 101. I had perfect skies and saw elephant seals, whale migration, many birds, and even Zebra...yes I know Zebra in California! (They are part of the cattle herds at Hearst Castle-which I finally enjoyed the tour of after years of just passing by)

I camped near the coast, enjoyed cold ocean breezes and hot summer-like days. The weather could not have been more perfect for the coastal stretch that has such variety. Even if I turned and rode it back down again the trip would give a completely different element that was not enjoyed on the first go round. That is the true beauty of travel in my eyes, even if you go to the same place...you never experience it in the same way.

It was also on Hwy 1 that I blew my daily budget with a $55.00 campsite, and it just blows my mind the price of camping today! It was a lovely site though and quiet in terms of people...but all my camping along the coast was always close enough to the ever popular highway that you still had the continuous car noise that brought back memories to my city life left just 3.5 weeks ago! It feels to be moving so quickly and slowly at the same time. I have heard the rhythm of the trip will find its tune at about a month and a half...so until then, I will ride and enjoy the journey of what the scenic roads and by-ways of the US have to offer!

## November 2014

### The Jaws of Life
*November 28, 2014 // 3 Comments*

It is the little things in life, truly that bring joy. And while on this trip I am beginning to feel the power of this age-old statement! Take for example these extra-large [...]

### KIVA - Thanksgiving beginning
*November 27, 2014 // 0 Comments*

For the past five years my Thanksgiving Holiday has been spent traveling and doing humanitarian work in developing countries. (which is a great reminder of all that I have to [...]

### NOLA
*November 25, 2014 // 1 Comment*

New Orleans Louisiana - is there a better place for a celebration of two months on the road! I stayed at a cute / quirky and affordable Historic Street Car Inn in the [...]

## Dichotomous Days
*November 25, 2014 // 0 Comments*

There are so many unique elements to the world of National Parks throughout the US, a big part of my journey is to visit and embrace as many as I can. And yes I have the [...]

## South Padre Island, TX
*November 24, 2014 // 3 Comments*

I moved around a lot growing up...and well...I guess I never grew out of it – but as a teenager in High School I spent a year in England and then moved to Texas [...]

## Street Stories – 1
*November 21, 2014 // 3 Comments*

The dark alleys, under the cardboard or curled in the overhangs of public doorways, the street corners or at the gas stations these are faces of the few we often forget and [...]

## Bear Essential News and Victoria Advocate
*November 21, 2014 // 1 Comment*

One of the things that I was not prepared for and have been humbled by is the young girls that are looking up to the story of my adventure and I must say that I am very [...]

ANELL LYNN

## Dumped!
*November 7, 2014 // 5 Comments*

Been Dumped...did I dump Amelia, or was I dumped...the age old question. The first time occurred due to the beauty of Mt. St. Helen's I completely blame it on [...]

## Episode 1 – The First Month
*November 5, 2014 // 1 Comment*

The first month was filled with many learning curves in technology, camera equipment, learning when and how to tape it all and create a mini - documentary for the first [...]

## You Can't Go Home Again
*November 3, 2014 // 2 Comments*

They say you can't go home again....so of course I did just that. A change in plans to be a part of a great project for the Arizona Production Association as we filmed a TV [...]

34

# You Can't Go Home Again

Posted on November 3, 2014 in Road Thoughts

They say you can't go home again...so of course I did just that.

A change in plans to be a part of a great project for the Arizona Production Association to film a TV Pilot gave me a new route to head home and visit the folks and my baby girl (yep my cat)! Pretty much the coolest cat – she is 13 and I have had her for that long. My parents are taking care of her while I am out on the road, and I have missed her dearly so was great to hangout!

There had been many technical issues on the road with learning the MAC I-Pad and figuring it all out...completely user error but it was nice to get back to my suitcase filled with alternative computer equipment. This enabled me to finish the formatting for my e-books (Philanthropic Wanderlust and Purposeful Wanderings) that had been on my to-do list for months now. I was able to get back to my stored portable hard drive to get into my "prep" videos and work on building my first webisode! It was fun and spent a good 7 hours one day and was not even halfway there – I am excited for the outcome!

Got caught up on my photo uploads, postings, and all that jazz! Was also greatly spoiled – you may have heard me mention my mother's cooking talents...but I received a variety of all homemade goodness. From Indian meals to a full mini-Thanksgiving and yes it included pie and dad's famous cranberry muffins! And of course nights of games from Farkel to Phase 10 and Rumi Cub!

This was a great needed multi-day break after 1.5 months on the road and I was able to re-tweak things and received my new warm winter liners from REV'IT so I am prepped and ready to head back out. And speaking of food – grandma set me up with a new load of dehydrated meals ready for the road (and the week before my aunt gave me some of their mushrooms that they gathered in northern AZ ). I know I am spoiled...

It has taken me a bit to get in the groove and my good friends that have taken these extended adventures have let me know after about the 1.5 month mark you feel in your element...and they are right – I am ready to depart south for the winter and take on a new adventure on paths I have never ridden!

# Episode 1 – The First Month

*Posted on November 5, 2014 Road Thoughts*

The first month was filled with many learning curves in technology, camera equipment, learning when and how to tape it all and create a mini – documentary for the first month on the road! It came together and was a lot of fun. Hope you enjoy!

https://youtu.be/mOMekfHZBTQ

# Dumped!

Posted on November 7, 2014

Been Dumped-did I dump Amelia, or was I dumped-the age old question.

The first time occurred due to the beauty of Mt. St. Helen's, I completely blame it on her! I had driven by a gorgeous view and stopped right after up the hill and pulled out of the lane – I cranked the wheel – should be an easy turn, I mean I was turning to go back down the hill. But as I cranked the wheel (completely stopped mind you) looked to make the turn, on this awesome spot to make a turn around, in a blind curve and bam – foot slips and I go down.

It was fast and all was good until I tried to get up and realized my foot that slipped went right under my saddle bag! All was good with the ankle as I have soft shell so it was padded but I could not pull it out! Begin a mild panic-here I sat in the middle of one lane, on a blind curve, and could not get my leg out – then the smell of gas-leaking and puddle next to me. So I took my right leg and began to move the bike by pushing (scratching my windshield as I huff and puff to push it off) and then I see a truck in the opposite lane. I causally wave from the ground-just an everyday hello and they pull off to come help me lift it up.

A woman jumped out first ran to me and once I told her I actually had ZERO mph and just fell over from a stopped position she yelled back to her father and uncle that I was okay. We got the bike up and then the father – probably in his 70's said to me, "can I ask you something personal?" I said, "yes for sure you just picked me up off the road!" "What kind of gun are you carrying, there are lots of crazies men out there!" I laugh and stated that I am okay and thanked them for their help. We all laughed and I got back to that beautiful picture spot, a little sorer than if I would have stopped the first time.

(This post was delayed in talking about as had to tell mom and dad in person to ease them into the post for when it happens again...and don't you know it the day I left their house on road to New Mexico...I got dumped again in the sand going to my wild campsite in Gila National Forest)

Had a great ride all day yesterday, skipped my wild camp spot in AZ as the National Forest spot had heavy gray clouds and it was still early so I rode on to NM. Riding up the 90 and into Gila National Forest I began to look for forest road turn outs for the perfect campsite! I found Gold Gulch road, and as I turned onto it there was what looked like a pedestrian path to the left and a wider road with truck tracks to the right...I went right and within 40 seconds quickly realized I was in a wash and the sand below my tires was getting deeper and was moist from recent rains- not mud but definite not the easiest-I should have gone left! I road on for a few feet and began to wobble. I attempted to save it with speed but all it did was speed up my second dumping of the trip! This time there would be no others coming to help lift, I was off the beaten path and tried to pick her up...once, twice...by the third time I looked up the hill saw a perfect camp spot and began to unload the weight. Once I had all the top bags off I set up the camera...I mean this is the stuff you have to tape...I hit record and walked over determined to pick Amelia up on the first attempt.

I planted my feet, got the proper posture, squatted and with a mighty grunt began to lift...it was working she was going and so was I – deeper into the soft sand. As my feet sank in I was maybe three inches from having her upright, and right on cue both calves began to rapidly cramp and were on fire. I could not lose the momentum so I got higher on the tip-toes and fought through the cramps....and then on the first go Amelia was upright! I was beaming and out of breath but was proud that in that sand I was able to do it. I could not wait to see the video and see how I really did, review my posture...and of course I must not have hit record hard enough- I missed it! My first big soft dirt dumping and lifting...ahh well there are always the memories...and the sore muscles this morning as a reminder.

**Adventurous Woman Amazes**

by Reporter Sarah Hoyer,
Bonillas Basic Curriculum

On Sept. 19 I met up with Danell Lynn at Bonillas Elementary. She was about to embark on a cross country adventure. Lynn is going to attempt to break a world record by traveling to all 50 states and Canada in the most amount of miles in one year. She is going to do this trip on her motorcycle, alone.

Lynn wrote a book called "Purposeful Wanderings," a nonfiction book about her life adventures. Lynn is an author and an adventurous young woman. I will only use one word to describe her: AWESOME!!!

When I heard I had a chance to interview her, I jumped at the opportunity. I

# Bear Essential News and Victoria Advocate

*Posted on November 21, 2014  News*

One of the things that I was not prepared for and have been humbled by is the young girls that are looking up to the story of my adventure and I must say that I am very honored!

 Take this story written by Sarah Hoyer from the first school I visited when this trip began. To be able to show young women – yes you can! And inspire young writers at the same time is quite amazing. Thank you Sarah for the great interview and lovely write up! Read the entire story here:
http://www.bearessentialnews.com/archives/2014/Nov14/scoopTucsonNov14.php

IN THE NEWS:

Another story that was featured this week was from my time going through Victoria, Texas. A historic town with many aged and beautiful buildings and Fossati's Delicatessen ( the oldest Deli in Texas-est. 1882 and is still operated by the same family!) I went through this lovely town on my 2 month anniversary and it was my last city stop in TX on my way to Louisiana.

See the story
here: https://www.victoriaadvocate.com/news/2014/
nov/18/woman-rides-cross-country-in-search-of-
worlds-reco/

# Street Stories – 1

Posted on November 21, 2014  Street Stories

In the dark alleys, under the cardboard or curled in the overhangs of public doorways, the street corners or at the gas stations, these are faces of the few we often forget and push to the back of our minds.

By choice or circumstance meet those women and men, and often children who make up *"Street Stories"* a documentary and photographic journey of the men and women living homeless on the streets of the US.

The compilation of the documentary and photo collection will not become a reality until long after I have completed my year-long journey, but I wanted to share with you – Toby, a homeless man and his dog on Bourbon Street!

Part of this journey is in the hand knitted hats, I was able to complete about 40 before I departed and my goal is to make sure that they are delivered to at least one homeless individual in each state. Toby picked a perfect green and beige that matched his jacket!

# South Padre Island, TX

*Posted on November 24, 2014*

I moved around a lot growing up, and well, I guess I never grew out of it. But as a teenager in High School I spent a year in England and then moved to Texas to finish out the last 3, and never once did I drive all the way to the coastal towns.

Now I have, I finally visited South Padre Island almost 15 years after living and leaving the state. Determined to make it through the unbelievable Texas winds and the encroaching "Arctic Blast" I arrived for a 2 day stay in the Deluxe Cabins of South Padre KOA. Deluxe – meaning I had a lovely little kitchen, a couch, table, linens on a real bed and a private bathroom and shower (no need to share the camp stalls) and TV where I learned of the storms mass and the week it would spend right in my planned path!

It was lovely, and right on the water – and the fact that I had to use the heater in normally 20 degree warmer town was not a bother because I had a heater and was not out camping in the 32 degree and sometimes lower nights that this weather front brought in.

So yes it was cold, but could it be a better time to have 2 days in a cabin? The Lodge# 1, named *Castle in the Sand,* faces the water and I opened all the blinds and enjoyed evenings watching the Pelicans fly in and swoop down picking through what would become their dinner! There is a gracefulness to the large birds – that is until they land on the water with more of a plop and it is a wonder how they ever get their fish with the amount force smacking into the waters!

Most KOA's are privately run but available through the US and Canada and you can find and look at the types of cabins, RV spot or tenting available throughout the nation. In just 2 months of my trip I have done tent camping in a KOA in Benbow-CA, *Kamping* Cabins in Alamagordo-NM, and a Deluxe Cabin in South Padre-TX and Victoria-TX. (you can find all of these wonderful stays and more at http://www.KOA.com with an interactive map of locations)

# Dichotomous Days

*Posted on November 25, 2014*

There are so many unique elements to the world of National Parks throughout the US, a big part of my journey is to visit and embrace as many as I can. And yes I have the National Park Passport Book...I am that excited little kid going into the visitors center to stamp my entry day for the magnificent natural culture that is America's National Parks!

The dichotomy that exist is as vast as the countryside itself. In just three days I went from above ground treasure to magical underground worlds. I started in New Mexico and then into Texas...

First up – the White Sands of New Mexico in the
Tularosa Basin are 275 sq miles of gypsum sand desert.
I did the sunset walking tour which is free and you learn
the history of the area and can walk the entire hour
barefoot if you would like, and as the sun goes down
man does it get cold! But before the walk began I hit the
dunes with a circular sled (pictured in my gallery online
the round green thing strapped to the bike) that KOA
Alamogordo loaned me – it was a blast!

The day before I was playing in the dunes and now at
700+ feet below the surface I am traveling into the
depths of Carlsbad Caverns, New Mexico. I left
Alamogordo early as I had a big ride planned and would
be traveling to my cousins in Alpine, TX. I had figured
about an hour and half to enjoy the site and then back
on the road. Once I turned on the 285 to head south the
winds kicked in, it was a good break to arrive at the
caverns. I bought my ticket (which is actually free-sort
of I have the $80 a year NP pass that has already paid
for itself in the 10+ parks and sites I have visited) and
turned the corner to head down only to be greeted by a
ranger on his walkie-talkie. He says to me, "Sorry the
electric just went out, we had to turn on the backup

DANELL LYNN

generator it should just be a short while." This turned
into 30 min. I was getting worried because I knew I only
had so much light to ride, so I ask again to another
woman, "oh not long, maybe fifteen minutes, maybe an
hour." An hour! So I took in the 17 min. free video and
had some lunch, and checked again. "Someone ran into
an electric pole outside the park they are trying to get
us back up and running."

This crazy wind probably threw someone off the road,
but how long would it be – do I stay and wait or leave to
be sure to get to my destination before dark? I decided
to use the restroom one more time and walk really
slowly...coming back in I heard a ranger tell another
couple that the rangers are in there making sure all
lights are functioning! Fantastic I turned to the
elevators with the other couple and by this time the
visitor center was packed but they had not made an
announcement on speakers just through walkie talkies
so we were the only three in the elevator. And as luck
would have it they had to use the restroom, so as I
entered and for the first 15 – 20 minutes I was the only
person in the caverns....the only noise was the dripping
water and the sound of my own footsteps! Not very
often you get a solo tour of Carlsbad Caverns, it was
wondrous and my pictures are people-less - definitely
worth the wait.

Then the next day back above land in Texas for
towering boulders and vast river carved mountain
crevasses of Big Bend National Park. It is a driving loop
to enter and exit the park with little roads that you can
take to end destinations (like the picture below) and it
was recommended to take the 22 mile road to the
canyon by the ranger as I entered.

I asked about gas and there was some about 70 miles in so I was good. It was completely worth it and a perfect day to visit. The day before they had some heavy rains and much of the road was flooded and covered with mud, I only had to cross dry mud and no roads were closed. As you travel through the loop of the main part of the park it is easy to put in 100 miles and you will see a variety from jagged rocks to canyons, hill like mountains and more...and not to be missed were the four tarantulas that crossed the roads as I rode through!

See more of these natural wonders in the BT2BT online photo gallery – Gallery Week 7 & 8-
http://www.BT2BT.smugmug.com

# NOLA

*Posted on November 25, 2014*

New Orleans Louisiana – is there a better place for a celebration of two months on the road!

I stayed at the cute / quirky and affordable Historic Street Car Inn in the Garden District and just a St. Charles Car Line ride from the French Quarter. A perfect little place and pleasing to the budget for a two night stay in New Orleans at only $53 a night!

Visiting the "oldest active City of the Dead" walking along paths washed from hurricane Katrina-they still have centuries of history and tales with stories as vast as the story tellers. I visited the tomb of Marie Laveau covered in xxx's and then around on another path "I visited the tomb of Marie Laveau covered in xxx's"...which is the real tomb depends on who you ask.

St. Louis Cemetery 1 was the first. The aged tombs I visited and the layouts of the cemeteries are truly worth a visit. I took in three different cemeteries while doing a walking tour of the French Quarter and Garden District. (St Louis Cemetery 1 and 2, and Lafayette Cemetery)

The Garden district was built-in the 1800's and shows its charm and magnificence in the large "southern style" homes that are said to, "rival the architectural splendor and beauty of the French Quarter." Walking through the streets you see the charm, and I imaged rocking chairs on porches filled with smiling bodies drinking sweet ice-tea. The elegance of the homes hold a lavishness that could be appealing in horror movies – such was the case as I strolled by a Major Motion picture "Crone (Abattoir)" thought to myself...wonder if they need a girl riding a motorcycle for any scene but did not work up the guts to walk up to production and ask...but was a fun thought none the less.

The French Quarter – the original city has a draw to travelers, artists and writers and its spell is not lost on me. The charm that Mark Twain reportedly admired in the city is definitely apparent. From Bourbon St. to St. Louis to Canal and Decatur, I walked it all! I saw many sights in one day and when I left my hotel that morning I did not come back until almost 8pm!

Jackson Square houses the oldest active "Catholic Church in America" – St. Louise Cathedral and is near where I would take in the tree lighting ceremony and concert. The 27 foot fleur-de-lis topped tree in Washington Artillery Park kicked off the feel for the season. The square was filled with free concerts and also got my caricature drawn with the bike! Garlands, lights and hot coco...a second helping of beignets from Cafe Du Monde...yes please!

See more photos on my BT2BT gallery page and my
NOLA VooDoo handmade string doll that now
accompanies me on my trip. I selected "Zombie Boy –
means no harm to anyone ... shield to protect from
anything harmful" and it is adorable so a fun treasure
from my time spent in NOLA (which by the way did not
hit me at first that it stands for New Orleans Louisiana –
a little slow on the uptake of that one ).

$9,975 of $10,000 to go

danell                    ENDING 9/20/15

## BT2BT - year journey

Nov 2014 Thankful – I am on the road adventuring through the US and Canada - all my belongings in storage, I am not in need for holidays - so for Christmas this year I am launching a KIVA campaign that will continue through my birthday and end on my year anniversary of Black Tie 2 Black Top Journey.

What is Kiva?

Support this campaign by lending to one of these borrowers.

Maria Angela            $50 to go

# KIVA –
# Thanksgiving beginning

*Posted on November 27, 2014*

For the past five years my Thanksgiving Holiday has been spent traveling and doing humanitarian work in developing countries. (which is a great reminder of all that I have to be thankful for)

When I am back home and want to feel connected as a global citizen I visit Kiva. I came across Kiva a few years ago and was hooked! For as little as $25 you can loan money to a person around the globe creating a business or rebuilding a home / hut...a little bit goes a very long way with Kiva and they are loans so they get repaid! I have always received repayment and when I do I choose to reinvest in another loan. ( I have loaned in 6 of the 84 countries they currently have available for loans – from

Bolivia to Cambodia, Tajikistan to Philippines, and more) I think it is always great fun – as you get to search through the site and get to know the person that you are loaning to! Check out www.Kiva.org

100% of your loan goes to funding the loan (during check out you can choose to provide funds to help run Kiva as well)

Kiva – "empower people around the world with $25" Many people around the holidays look for gifts with meaning, and it definitely is that and has an over 98% repayment rate.

*"We envision a world where all people – even in the most remote areas of the globe – hold the power to create opportunity for themselves and others.*

*We believe providing safe, affordable access to capital to those in need, Kiva helps people create better lives for themselves and their families."*

Kiva gives you the chance to make small loans to borrowers working to start businesses and improve their lives. I'm already lending on Kiva and thought you'd like to join me! I have decided this holiday season to start a Kiva Campaign ( a new way from Kiva to build a team and goal of loans for a certain amount of time). I am starting mine this Thanksgiving and letting it run throughout the last 10 months of my trip...10 months – with a goal of $10,000 in loans around the globe- A fun way to incorporate giving and charity into my trip – both of which are very important to me!

(**I did not make my goal, but some very wonderful people became KIVA givers and I am thankful for their hearts and generosity**)

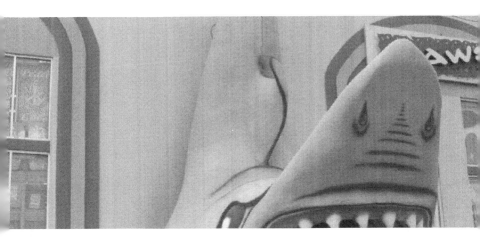

# The Jaws of Life

*Posted on November 28, 2014*

It is the little things in life, truly that bring joy. And while on this trip I am beginning to feel the power of this age-old statement!

Take for example these extra-large shark heads...I saw this one on the coast Mississippi and another that I was trying to reverse into...it would have been a perfect pic in South Padre but the woman at the store came out and said NO! I thought oh great

57

could you at least take my picture on the bike in front...NO again...oh well, was still awesome to put Amelia into so many Shark heads!

And now I am in Florida and only time will tell if she will get photographed in yet another Jaws moment.

## December 2014

### Best Kiss in Florida...
*December 17, 2014 // 1 Comment*

The vastness of terrain and life in Florida makes for many memories and photographs. A not to be missed chance is snorkeling with the Manatee's in the fresh springs [...]

### 4 days, 3 nights, and 15 mosquito bites...
*December 10, 2014 // 2 Comments*

Welcome to camping in the Everglades! Ask me if it is worth it and I will tell of my first night falling asleep to the sound of insects and waking up to the calls of birds! [...]

# 4 days, 3 nights, and 15 mosquito bites…

*Posted on December 10, 2014*

Welcome to camping in the Everglades! Ask me if it is worth it and I will tell of my first night falling asleep to the sound of insects and waking up to the calls of birds! Finally, no traffic noise, no loud music, almost 3 months in and I had the camping I had been craving all trip!

My first day in Everglades National Park was pretty magical as well, and best described by a call I made home…hello mom and dad, "so I can't feel my left arm, got a slight sunburn, bug bites, am completely exhausted and ABSOLUTELY loved it! – I kayaked for four hours, over 10+ miles down a canal, into a windy lake, through overgrown pass-through (had to duck

under trees – the true Everglades) and made it to Mud
Lake! Had a blast, just wanted to share my crazy day."

I built campfires from wood I collected and used a
couple of logs as well, I practiced my harmonica by the

light of the fire until the bugs would cause my retreat
into my tent were I would devour books on kindle in the
night while serenaded by the flutter and ticking of
nature's own rhythm. I copied down Amazons list of
100 books to read in your lifetime and the first
completed off that list *Born to Run* a  great read! And
now onto a mystery/thriller not on the list and a little
Hemingway to prepare for the Key West visit to
Hemingway's house! Which will be fun as last summer I
went to his house in Cuba.

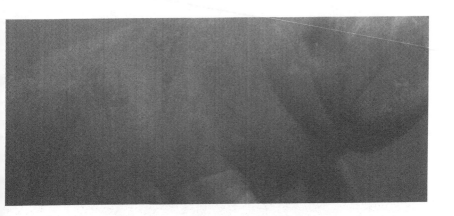

# Best Kiss in Florida...

*Posted on December 17, 2014*

The vastness of terrain and life in Florida makes for many memories and photographs. A not to be missed chance is snorkeling with the Manatee's in the fresh springs throughout the state!

I did the swim in Crystal River, and although it was an unseasonable cold day with fog and at only 38 degrees, I excitedly jumped into the water (which sits at about 74 degrees). Sounds warm but after a while you shiver uncontrollably...but completely worth it when the gentle giant swims right at you and comes to your face for a manatee kiss! This is actually them seeing you better through touch from their whiskers and is a wonderful experience!

The visibility was not the best so often I did not know they were there until I felt a bump on my knee or side, and then if you slowly put your hand out and pet them they turn around and come back for more! They love their belly rubbed!

This is something I would definitely do again and again and some houses sit right on the river...how wonderful would that be to just wake up have your coffee, have a swim with the Manatee's, spend the day writing, and maybe have a swim again! I think maybe I could do that!

DANELL LYNN

## January 2015

### Winter Weather
*January 31, 2015 // 0 Comments*

In an advert for heated gear I once read "because nature has mood swings." And oh how true that has been this winter! I have either been running from or hiding [...]

### Texas Press
*January 30, 2015 // 4 Comments*

Two news stations in Texas – Thank you KTAB and KTXS. (they have the same pic on you-tube but two different coverages.) Both less than a minute long – enjoy! [...]

### The Sounds of Camping
*January 29, 2015 // 1 Comment*

It's 2am and the screeching wakes me – with a quickened heartbeat and slow shallow breaths! I sit up, pull my ears out of my sock hat, and push down my mummy [...]

### El Camino
*January 27, 2015 // 1 Comment*

Dreams are always changing and to see my home country from the backroads and travel through farmland and desolate communities is magnificent and humbling at the same time. [...]

## Disintegration Dilemma
*January 23, 2015 // 5 Comments*

As far back as I can remember the disintegration of things past has always held a beauty for me. As a young teen I would go out and take pictures of dead plants, or peeling [...]

## Episode 3 – Month 3
*January 11, 2015 // 5 Comments*

The journey continues east and an extended stay in Florida. Now live Episode 3 – Month 3. Enjoy the vast open roads and underwater explorations, from alligators to [...]

## Elvis' 80th
*January 9, 2015 // 0 Comments*

Feels fitting to do my post about my December visit to Graceland today – on Elvis' birthday – he would have been 80. Riding into Memphis on the 19th of [...]

## Triumphant Dealers
*January 5, 2015 // 3 Comments*

Being a solo female riding a Triumph around the nation gets looks – often of concern, occasionally of doubt, and sometimes grand looks of understanding and support for [...]

## The Barber Honor
*January 4, 2015 // 1 Comment*

Traveling into Birmingham, AL to visit the Barber Vintage Motorcycle Museum – I was expecting an amazing viewing but received even more and a honor while there! I had [...]

## The Barber Honor

*January 4, 2015 // 1 Comment*

Traveling into Birmingham, AL to visit the Barber Vintage Motorcycle Museum - I was expecting an amazing viewing but received even more and a honor while there! I had [...]

## Home for the Holidays!

*January 1, 2015 // 3 Comments*

I have often spent Christmas away from my family as an adult - mostly while traveling out of country and working with Threading Hope and Highwire - but this year [...]

# Home for the Holidays!

*Posted on January 1, 2015*

I have often spent Christmas away from my family as an adult – mostly while traveling out of country and working with Threading Hope and Highwire – but this year being stateside it was hard not to be home for the traditions. Mom's homemade cinnamon rolls and dad's Christmas chili! So with only 6 days until Christmas I decided to head home for the Holidays.

Riding from Florida to Arizona in 6 days made for a heck of a journey. After winds and a bit exhausted I spent half a day in Roswell, NM and got some fun Alien local brew for the family. The next day was cold and snow warnings throughout my path – so I took the high road where snow was not in the forecast...but as I found out – Ice was!

I have learned to laugh at moments that might otherwise bring stress, but going down at slow speed while trying to record my "great ice riding skills" is simply humorous! Even though under 5 mph my shield was shattered in the fall because it was frozen! I was fine, landing on my hip pads in my Rev'It gear was a comfort and left me with no bruising!

The Ice fall was a surprise but the bigger surprise was not 10 minutes down the hill and out of the ice now into sunlight, and who comes around the corner. As I attempted to gas up-no no not Santa and 8 tiny reindeer but who else but my dad on his own two wheels! It was awesome and the extra set of hands to help with the duct tape fix until I could metal stitch the shield was definitely welcomed! We had a blast riding the last 400+ miles back to Tucson, AZ for a family filled holiday celebration!

# The Barber Honor

*Posted on January 4, 2015*

Traveling into Birmingham, AL to visit the Barber Vintage Motorcycle Museum – I was expecting an amazing viewing but received even more and a honor while there! I had read about this little gem in the AMA magazine earlier this year and met up with one of my motorcycle world traveling friends to view the awesome collection.

Down in the restoration area there sits two columns. These pillars are not only for support but are filled with signatures by visitors from the likes of Jay Leno, Evil Knievel, Richard Petty, Johnny Rutherford, Craig Vetter...and they asked if I would join the list! What an honor, and wonderful for them to have the same belief in me that I will break the record. Thank you so much! (and watch out for the episode 3 – month 3 webisode-this will be featured there!)

If you don't know of this museum, I hope this write-up inspires a visit: *"Home to the world's best motorcycle collection, the museum now has over 1200 vintage and modern motorcycles and racecars and the largest collection of Lotus cars as well as other significant makes. The collection is the largest of its kind in the world. There are approximately 600 of the 1200 motorcycles on display at any given time. These bikes range from 1902 to current-year production. The museum displays common street bikes as well as rare one-off Gran Prix race machinery."*

I had a wonderful time and not only is the collection impressive but the staff are well educated in the history that these walls hold. See more pictures in the gallery – http://bt2bt.smugmug.com/Barbers-Vintage-Motors/

# Triumphant Dealers

*Posted on January 5, 2015*

Being a solo female riding a Triumph around the nation gets looks – often of concern, occasionally of doubt, and sometimes grand looks of understanding and support for my year-long undertaking. The supportive looks have come in 3's over the last 15,000 miles.

I have had great support and honest maintenance from coast to coast and the central US. Even though on a solo-expedition I have found partners in the Triumph Dealerships across the nation.

There are 3 in particular that stand out due to great service, great work, and all around great people!

My first grand stop was at Triumph of Tacoma. A very organized shop and service area. I felt nothing but welcome and they took great care of me not only getting my new tires on and rear brake pads but they did a full look over to make sure I was good to go! They made the process easy and all I had to do was drop off Amelia and enjoy the ride!

Fast forward to my 10,000 mile marker on the road! I was visiting my great aunt in Florida and met the great guys of BMW Ducati Triumph of Daytona. By this time I had a broken side panel from high winds in TX & NM and just had it held on with duct-tape, I had burned through another set of tires...and what I received was beyond – above and beyond! Not only did I learn that plastic can be welded (and the service manager actually showed me the new tools and taught me how it works) so they fixed my side panel, did value adjustments, lubed and checked everything, unbent my kickstand, discounted my new set of tires and just blew me away with kindness and willingness to be a part of my adventure.

I learned at the Dayton shop that in about 5000 miles I would need to replace my chain and sprocket, and determined to get the most I could out of it- I rode on...Amelia had another thought. At about 14,500 just hitting El Paso, TX heading back to the East and staying south for the winter – I stopped for gas and was welcomed with a new noise from my front tire...was it a tire flat-nope, was it the break pads-not sure, the odo cable-nope...I made it .8 miles to a hotel and took it to Viva Powersports the very next morning. I had not heard this noise before and wanted to learn what it was.

They were willing to let me be in the bay and work through it with them. Diagnostic began and after ruling out my first few thoughts, they then moved to looking into the bearings...and yep a bad front wheel bearing! Did I mention this occurred on New Years Eve so getting parts around the holidays meant delays. They were great about it though and also offered to update my chain and sprocket and fix the front bearings, so I found a hotel and was glad to outstay the ice rain storms and tornados that were in my path east anyways, was a needed break and gave me writing time while they took care of Amelia!

Thanks greatly to the amazing relationships I have had thus far 4 months, 15 states and almost 15,000 miles on the road with Triumph dealerships! Cheers to you guys!

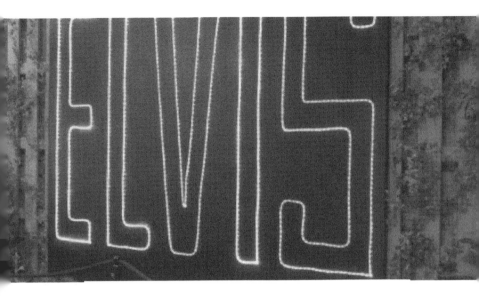

# Elvis' 80th

Posted on January 9, 2015

Feels fitting to do my post about my December visit to Graceland today – on Elvis' birthday – he would have been 80.

Riding into Memphis on the 19th of December, a good friend of mine (fellow motorbike rider) and I visited Graceland, I on my Triumph, he on his new BMW.  It was made special not only because of where it was, Graceland, but in landing there on my 3 months on the road anniversary!  We got to walk through the Mansion, his airplanes, the car museum and more...it was great.

The thing I did not know about Elvis was all the charity work that he did, I knew of some but not to the extent I do now. There are those that change the world with their fame as Elvis did, and those that use their fame to change the world and make it better – as I now know Elvis also did!

It is quite odd when you first arrive as the mansion just sits right off a main road – and you park on the other side and take a bus right across the street. It is a dance they have learned well and coordinated with the thousands of visitors each year.

I grew up listening to "oldies" Rock and Roll and have danced to Elvis more often than not, his music just gets into you and the rhythm flows ...you get a little shake whether you mean to or not! Happy 80th!

More pictures on the BT2BT gallery pages – week 13!

Loved this picture in one of the old buildings – the outdoor studio / office area.

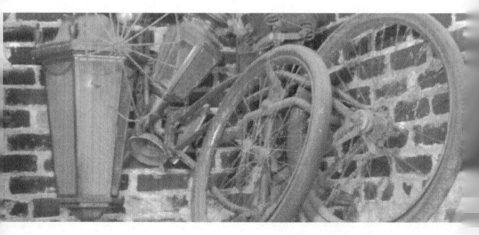

# Episode 3 – Month 3

*Posted on January 11, 2015*

The journey continues east and an extended stay in Florida. Now live Episode 3 – Month 3. Enjoy the vast open roads and underwater explorations, from alligators to manatee kisses to roadside fires...

Check out the youtube video:

**https://youtu.be/IIOuodtV2zs**

# Disintegration Dilemma

Posted on January 23, 2015

As far back as I can remember the disintegration of things past have always held a beauty for me. As a young teen I would go out and take pictures of dead plants, or peeling dead bark on old trees. This grew into a love toward old buildings no longer able to be a home but the structure still strong and filled with experiences, stories and history!

Maybe it is a metaphor of sorts for life – as we age our structure breaks down but there is still such beauty and life held within. I am not sure exactly what draws me to these buildings but I find myself photographing them often on this journey.

Whether condemned buildings boarded up in the
Florida Keys or falling down historical properties in
New Orleans, to the outskirts of Natchez, MS where I
found the amazing old barns and buildings for the
photographs in this blogpost – I am endlessly drawn to
them.

See more pictures of Louisiana and Mississippi in –
Gallery-Week 17–

# El Camino

Posted on January 27, 2015

Dreams are always changing and to see my home country from the backroads and travel through farmland and desolate communities is magnificent and humbling at the same time.

One of the roads that held both these elements and so much more was the US Highway 84 – El Camino 5-State East/West Corridor. At 1,729 miles long it stretches from El Paso, TX through LA, MS, AL, and into GA.

While traveling through TX the ride is a historic older part called the El "Camino Real" in Spanish – translated to "The Kings Highway" named after the historic trail that connected to Mexico as part of old settlement routes. The road today varies from rolling hills of farmlands, grazing cattle and horses, to open roads for helmet-time contemplation, to tree lined empty paths (I was often the only person on the road for long periods of time) to the occasional friendly fellow biker wave that always puts a smile on my face.

Having ridden this path through all 5 states it is a road I can say with confidence is worth a ride! I thoroughly enjoyed the path and journey it took me down!

# The Sounds of Camping

*Posted on January 29, 2015*

It's 2am and the screeching wakes me – with a quickened heartbeat and slow shallow breaths! I sit up, pull my ears out of my sock hat, and push down my mummy sleeping bag so as not to block my ability to hear how close this pack of coyotes might be!

They were in the camp – close but another campers dog scared them-or alerted the owners and they scared them away-me well I sat awake for another hour envisioning the thin walls of my tented home and how quickly a hungry pack could easily find me. I was one of 2 tents, the rest RV campers and the other tent campers at least had their hunting truck.

Alas not all noises quicken the heart, many slow it way down. One of the most special sounds is natures lullaby to sleep. Filled with joys of clicking insect wings, and before dusk settles the birds that help put the world to rest. Within the hour of darkness – silence sets in-as if to say "goodnight world-rest well" and usually I do!

Occasionally you get the odd squirrel feet running across the top of the tent, after a thud as they jump / fall from the trees! Thank goodness the sun had already crested or this moment of humor and fascination just watching these little feet go back and forth in a manic manor trying to find a way down. If it had been dark and I was unable to see what caused the noise in an active imagination this could easily been another heart pounding moment!

I tend to go to bed with the light, as the sun goes down I venture into my tent, pull out my Kindle and read until I fall asleep. No sounds of alarms, no pressure to depart my day or wake up for the next, just the pure essence of circadian rhythms reminding me when to rest and when to wake.

# Texas Press

*Posted on January 30, 2015*

Riding through Abilene, Texas where I went to high school I was greeted with a great reception from the local news crews.

Two news stations in Texas – Thank you KTAB and KTXS. (they have the same pic on you-tube but two different coverages.) Both less than a minute long – enjoy!

https://youtu.be/JOu9dnGQzJg

https://youtu.be/LLpASycu-AA

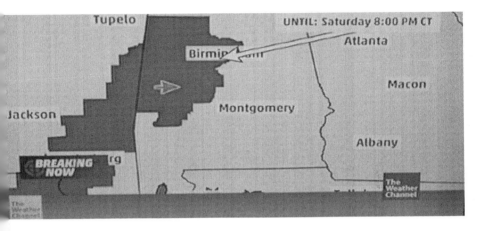

# Winter Weather

*Posted on January 31, 2015*

In an advert for heated gear I once read "because nature has mood swings." And oh how true that has been this winter!

I have either been running from or hiding within these "Winter Storm Warnings" all named –from Frona to Iola and Arctic Blasts to Nor-Easters'. I have had them all in the south as the entire country has had it – record lows for winter in many areas since the late 1800's! Crazy! It has had me held up indoors longer than expected at times, but also finding pride in the courage of tent camping in these odd winter conditions. I do have to say I added an old army issue wool blanket to the kit as I could not stay warm with just the sleeping bag and liner. (thanks to mom and dad for the lend of this much-needed comfort) I also now ride in heated gear!

I am okay getting out of the rain or weather and enjoying a hotel stay! It has been a joy camping in so many states, I hope to plant tent pegs in every state – thus far 10 of the 15 I have visited I have camped in (2 of the 15 were just drive thru that I will definitely revisit) The weather has effected when and where I can camp for example the most recent venture through the El Camino Corridor I camped in TX, LA, MS, but had to hotel in AL as Iona hit, so I will hit AL as I loop back at some point. Part of the joy is the ability of an open trip to be able to say that – I will just figure it later and loop back in!

Weather has not taken away anything in my journey thus far and as I have said in response when chatting with people met on the road who question my thoughts in "traveling at this time of year" –When traveling for a year-winter will hit no matter what time of year I would have departed, that is the consistency of season – winter occurs every year...as does spring and summer which currently I look forward to for the northern states!

## February 2015

### A warm welcome on a Snowy day

*February 25, 2015 // 2 Comments*

Waking up to a snowy morning in Pinetop – Lakeside, Arizona... a cold start but a wonderfully warm welcome in Mrs. Denise Green's elementary class for a day [...]

### Valentines Sunsets and Bike Bonding

*February 14, 2015 // 3 Comments*

Sharing a sunset with the one you hold a bond – that is what Valentines Day is all about-right? It has been said that a line of crazy falls near to talking to [...]

### Eating Local

*February 11, 2015 // 0 Comments*

When I travel internationally I always try to experience the culture down to the level of foods eaten. It is fun to try new foods and experience different ways of eating old [...]

## Triumph Family
## Art in a Cow Pasture
*February 4, 2015 // 0 Comments*

Spending a week in Madison, Georgia was a gem of history and enjoyment. My time was filled with touring old southern homes, historic museums, and an art museum situated in [...]

### Turbulence of Tires
*February 6, 2015 // 5 Comments*

Until this journey I had not experienced the joy of feeling a tire blow out and puncture flats, nor had I before glowed from the pride of safely riding the flat and wobble to [...]

## Photo Shoots
*February 5, 2015 // 0 Comments*

A week of photo shoots started out with Design & Build Magazine. We took over the center of the street in downtown Madison, GA and took photos over the railroad tracks! I [...]

## The Solo Path

*February 2, 2015 // 4 Comments*

An unexpected rawness in emotions has become my passenger. I was not prepared to feel...to really feel all my emotions so strongly. Is it the journey, or the time to sit [...]

## Episode 4 – Month 4

*February 2, 2015 // 0 Comments*

The journey continues... Here is the newest episode Month 4 (and below is Episode 3 incase you missed it)   Episode 3 – Month 3 on the [...]

OVER 15000 MILES, 15 STATES, 4 MONTHS...

# Episode 4 – Month 4

*Posted on February 2, 2015*

The journey continues...

Here is the newest episode Month 4 -
https://youtu.be/zuCaDa2YhBo

# The Solo Path

*Posted on February 2, 2015*

An unexpected rawness in emotions has become my passenger. I was not prepared to feel, to really feel all my emotions so strongly. Is it the journey, or the time to sit and contemplate? Is it the time spent without speaking to anyone – often days at a time? Or is it just the trip itself and the outcome a journey of this magnitude creates.

Some of the emotions are wonderful and freeing and others are just down right odd, and even in the mists of feeling them I wonder – what the hell! Take for example when I was trying to meet up with friends and missed taking a picture I really wanted...I was so frustrated that it brought tears, over a missed photo! Instead of just turning around and riding back the hour I called home to say "what the hell – why am I so emotional, I am crying over a photo"...mom was great and said to just go back... "just go back!" Such a simple statement and although I knew I would – for some reason I had to cry it out first – so wiping away the weird tears I turned around and went back for one of my favorite photos to date!

That is just one of many examples of the rawness that occurs, one that is a little more on the "glass half full" side of life is the pure euphoria that I felt just in my slow breaths as I enjoyed the stunning sunsets over the lake between LA and TX during my time at North Toledo State Park camping. The colors in the sky seemed more vibrant and the sounds of the birds saying goodnight to the day seemed a pure, true fit to the elements surrounding me -nature wise and emotion wise!

And then there is the joy that even in the memories brings a smile to my face from such experiences such as kissing the Manatees. A true gentle giant that I am still very much in awe of!

These emotions – the raw tears, deep joy, soothing calmness – I welcome them all as part of the journey and cherish them even in the tears and the laughter that comes after when I question – "what was that?"

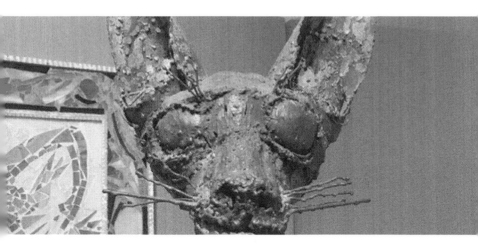

# Art in a Cow Pasture

*Posted on February 4, 2015*

Spending a week in Madison, Georgia was a gem of history and enjoyment. My time was filled with touring old southern homes, historic museums, and an art museum situated in the middle of a cow pasture in Buckhead, GA.

Steffen Thomas, was a talented artist in many mediums, well known around the world for his mosaic and sculpture, as well as for his "hat ladies" in paint.

Born in Germany and spending most of his life in Atlanta, Georgia he apprenticed as a young teen with a stonecutter, he was gifted and well taught as an artist and a poet!

I have had a postcard of one his painting since I was teen, and little did I know I would visit the town where his daughter lives and the museum of his work is housed. I was captivated by his mosaic sailboat kitchen table that has short legs and sits low to the ground, and the cat sculpture rendered as a celebration of the family cat named "Peter" there were works based on all the family cats -and yes they all had the same name...Peter the first, Peter the second...

His work and his lifestyle was touched by the expressionist notions. His work can be compared to Picasso and some seems touched and drafted with the same hands but then others stand on their own in strength of talent. It is a great little gem off a little highway in the middle of a cow pasture!

photo by Triumph America

# Photo Shoots

*Posted on February 5, 2015*

A week of photo shoots started out with *Design & Build Magazine*. We took over the center of the street in downtown Madison, GA and took photos over the railroad tracks! I look forward to seeing the outcome!

Then the next day was the *Morgan County Citizen* photo shoot for upcoming article in the newspaper! And the day after that another newspaper came out to shoot for a profile piece by Richard Hodgetts for the *Lake Oconee News* which covers, Green and Morgan Counties.

It will be great to see these all come out in print, one of my favorite things is seeing the creative spin that media takes and does with the story. I was elated for these three shoots and then I went to visit Triumph

95

Headquarters in Atlanta, to meet the Triumph North America family (blog to follow). While there I was asked if I had time for a photo shoot while in Georgia.

I stayed on an extra day for the photo shoot with Keith May for Triumph America. We had a blast shooting around the Mason property with over 200 years of history.

I will depart Georgia having had a wonderful time and many unplanned joys. I will head west, the plan was east coast but with 10 degree below normal temps for the next 10 days and in the west 8-10 degrees above normal I will head back and take in the camping in AL, AR, and OK that I did not get in yet- and maybe a few days in Nashville if the nights stay nice for walking around town and hearing all the local bands!

# Turbulence of Tires

*Posted on February 6, 2015*

Until this journey I had not experienced the joy of feeling a tire blow out and puncture flats. Nor had I before glowed from the pride of safely riding the flat and wobble to the shoulder and not falling over.

I knew this trip would have so many "firsts" for me but having my first and second rear flats – I can say with confidence it will be okay if those are the only two times I have these experiences! Not only are they what must be causing the new gray hairs I have popping up but the price of flats over the wear and tear from riding is just not so appealing! (5 rear tire replacements in less than 5 months- I am okay without the flats for sure!)

I often will just get in a groove on the road and it causes

a moment of panic..."was that a wobble?" Then I bounce out of the groove and take a deep breath.

Flats in both California and Texas, I cannot complain about them – truly as they both occurred in amazing locations. Close to my destinations and near dealerships... considering some of the roads I travel for hundreds of miles between cities and rarely seeing other drivers. It could have occurred in not so great conditions. So if it has to occur I have been blessed in the locations and time / date they occur somebody is keeping an eye out and all I can say is, "thank you, and it would be okay to no longer have a flat!"

# Triumph Family

*Posted on February 9, 2015*

When it is talked about "your family" on the road, I can't help but feel that my desire for Amelia – a Triumph Bonneville being the definite right bike for me. In meeting the Triumph family, at the North America Headquarters in Atlanta, I felt a wonderful welcome and knew why this bike felt like family from the start.

People at Triumph headquarters did not ask "why", they knew the why to a trip like this and they understood that the "why" is not always clear or of dramatic depth. Sometimes the why is simply the desire... the need to just get on Amelia and ride!

It was always the difficulty before I took a year off – I

DANELL LYNN

would ride Amelia to work – only to find I hated
stopping on the ride home and just wanted to keep
going. And sometimes I did. I only lived 4 miles from the
office so I would take the long way home some days and
add a 50 to 60 mile commute loop before taking off the
helmet!

Many people during my visit had similar stories and
desires. It was also great to see the history lining the
walls of vintage Triumph posters and current celebrities
that have used the bikes in films or in music videos! It is
an office but feels more like a walking fine art collection
of Triumph – what a neat desk / work space to come
into each day!

Very glad to have met with so many smiling faces and
really felt like a welcome home- so cheers for that
Triumph-! And big shout out to Todd for the great tour
and the history of so many stories, and to Beth for
connecting us all and Jessica for making the tour
happen. Really had a wonderful time! See you all out on
the road!

# Eating Local

*Posted on February 11, 2015*

When I travel internationally I always try to experience the culture down to the level of foods eaten. It is fun to try new foods and experience different ways of eating old foods. Just like my travels abroad, on this trip around my home country, I wanted to eat local area foods.

The United States is a vast and diverse country- from landscapes, to culture, to food. I have enjoyed trying to get local eats in the places I visit and have had great luck in the south thus far. From traditional key lime pie in Key West, to fried catfish and lima beans in Mississippi, collard greens and fried pickles in Memphis, TN and grits in northern and southern Florida, kind of like Italy the way they eat it in the north differs from the sugar and milk in the south!

DANELL LYNN

As well as old loves like cafe con leche in Miami and
Pastilitos in Florida City! Not to mention the grapefruit
sized avocados in Florida with the beautifully buttery
texture and so much delicious avocado meat more than
3 cups in each side!

I have been getting such variety and great foods, but I
do miss on the road...my blended shakes filled with
greens, chai, fruit, veggies, seeds, figs, etc...an entire
mixed variety that changes every time depending on if
an after workout mix or just a mid-day hunger fix! I
miss that meal / food the most!

I cannot wait to see what local finds I might get
traveling the eastern shores! Cheers to great eats – see
you on the road!

# Valentines Sunsets and Bike Bonding

*Posted on February 14, 2015*

Sharing a sunset with the one you hold a bond – that is what Valentine's Day is all about-right?

It has been said that a line of crazy falls near to talking to oneself...what then is to become of talking to one's motorbike?

You go through a lot, trials and joys, beauty and darkness, and you build a bond unlike any with another of soul or emotion. It is odd to build a bond with an object but when you travel solo and you just kicked butt on that road and hit the dirt curves and stayed upright-your cheers just might be a tank pat and often in my case a "well done Amelia!" I need my cheerleaders of my trip and thus I am Amelia's cheerleader!

We are a pair not bonded with a relationship of souls but bonded with the need for adventure. She was not built for this type of ride I heard, she is a street bike... you cannot go at it alone...as a woman...it is crazy! We bonded in the joy of breaking what we are not to do! (something I have found pleasure often disproving what "can't" be done, I think I was born with that gene of defiance of standard "shoulds" or preconceptions).

We have been with each other every day through 16 states and 17000 miles, through rain, snow, ice, sweat inducing hot days, and shivering cold days! We have ridden on dirt, gravel, asphalt, and a kind of combination road and made it out! She has been my rock when I feel overly emotional and has also been my cause of emotion on the road!

We are bonded, this trip has bonded me to a bike – my Triumph Amelia and I ride – we are one on the road, and take in both hands and on both wheels the adventure that is ahead of us!

# A warm welcome on a Snowy day

Posted on February 25, 2015

Waking up to a snowy morning in Pinetop – Lakeside, Arizona, a cold start but a wonderfully warm welcome in Mrs. Denise Green's elementary class for a day of cultural and travel discussions!

I brought my Cultural Coloring books to donate a classroom set to the students – each getting their very own and an extra for the teacher that she can make copies from for any lesson she would like! We talked about travel and the gifts it gives back, we had discussions for over 40 minutes based directly on cultural exploration and humanitarianism. After our talks it was time to color! A lovely gesture when one of the students asked me to sign their books and then they all lined up. I wrote a personal message and chatted individually with each child - it made the morning that much more special.

This class was a perfect fit for me to visit as community service is a part of their curriculum. We talked about the work they have done and the work I have done with Highwire and Threading Hope. We had surprisingly philosophical discussions that blew me out of the water with the questions coming from such young minds (they are only in 3rd grade and very dedicated to making the world a better place).

Thank you to Blue Ridge Elementary for hosting me and Mrs. Green for inviting me into her class, and most of all thank you to the students who are out there making the world that much better to live in!

# 1 Woman, 1 Motorbike, 1 Year

## March 2015

### Where do you go...
*March 29, 2015 // 2 Comments*

Working on my article for 2 Wheeled Wanderlust the Magazine for the Spring / Summer issue out in May and I couldn't help but find myself thinking... Where do I go [...]

### The Bill Factor
*March 27, 2015 // 11 Comments*

I was getting new AVON tires and was quite excited! I called up Bill and Susan Dragoo and asked if I could send them to their house and were they up for a visit – I was [...]

### Taste of Dakar
*March 16, 2015 // 1 Comment*

So I was right off the strip in a hotel of Las Vegas and got a call that I should come out into the deserts of Pahrump, NV! I grabbed the bike rode through the Red Rock [...]

### Episode 5
*March 11, 2015 // 2 Comments*

Magical moments in Nashville, and my first ever "tagging" just happens to be on a Cadillac! From covered wooden bridges in Georgia to snow covered mountain roads [...]

### The People we Meet
*March 10, 2015 // 1 Comment*

In an extended journey one meets many people, some just in passing and some that will stay with you for years to come. Many of the people I meet are only for one day, [...]

## Bluegrass on the Beach

*March 9, 2015 // 1 Comment*

Funny that I have lived in Arizona the last 8 years and just attended the 13th annual Lake Havasu – Bluegrass on the Beach Music Festival...better late than never! [...]

## Ghost Towns and Wild Burros

*March 6, 2015 // 0 Comments*

Leaving Kingman, AZ with a beautiful drive through the historic side of the city filled with murals, and vintage style gas pumps... drive a little further take a right [...]

# Ghost Towns and Wild Burros

Posted on March 6, 2015

Leaving Kingman, AZ with a beautiful drive through the historic side of the city filled with murals, and vintage style gas pumps...drive a little further and take a right onto Old Route 66, continue through a stunning ride into the mountains for a visit to the old mining town of Oatman, AZ.

A historic mining town centered around the gold rush of the 1800's and now draws people to the joy of a "Ghost Town" -although there are shops and tourist items -it is a very touristy area but is filled with a charm all its own. Making a mark with the "Wild Burro's" that roam the streets. (the burros roam but are familiar with the crowds of people that venture in, thus letting you feed and pet them)

Watch a high-noon gun fight between bank robbers or filter in and out of the antique shops...to be noted if you are coming in during the shootout and hit the Saloon for lunch you will wait over an hour. So if not much time it would be an ideal little town for a picnic!

And if you are lucky you may see the Burros take to the street for a duel, they did this a couple times-just be sure to be out of the way of those kicking back legs. Although they are used to people they are still a wild animal!

See more pictures of Oatman in BT2BT online Gallery – http://bt2bt.smugmug.com/Oatman-AZ-Ghost-Town/

# Bluegrass on the Beach

*Posted on March 9, 2015*

Funny that I have lived in Arizona the last 8 years and just attended the 13th annual Lake Havasu – Bluegrass on the Beach Music Festival...better late than never!

It was a perfect break from the cold eastern temperatures! I rode back west to spend a couple of days camping on the Colorado and then enjoying live music on the lake! This trip has reminded me how much I truly enjoy live music...from Nashville to Key West, and now Lake Havasu... I definitely need more live music in my life!

Some great bands held the line up from Monroe Crossing to The Spinney Brothers and the show closer on Saturday night – Blue Highway (pictured as the feature image of this post) and not to be forgotten – the stunning sunsets!

# The People we Meet

*Posted on March 10, 2015*

In an extended journey one meets many people, some just in passing and some that will stay with you for years to come. Many of the people I meet are only for one day, others I am lucky enough to ride with for multiple days, some for breakfast and some from the Triumph Team that service my Amelia and keep her safe on the road.

The internet has opened a new world to the last couple generations unlike anything else in our past. It is amazing that I can chat with people from Canada or across the pond in Europe and have well wishes from around the world (this blog is currently read in more than 74 countries and over 15,500 readers).

Many of the people I meet on the road are due to the internet, others met organically at gas stations. The best chance meetings in life are the ones that change you – for the better! The ones you learn from and carry with you! I have been lucky enough to experience this throughout my trip.

On an extended solo-trip it is often quite solitary and meeting people makes for some pretty great conversations. One of my favorite passerby moments was a young man I met at the gas station – he saw my windshield and we started chatting – he had a large U-haul and was on his way from Florida to a small farm in Arkansas to live a simpler life! I felt affinity for his life choice and he for mine – it was just a moment in time but it resonates!

So cheers to the unexpected and letting your heart and mind be open to new experiences and new connections. Thank you world for such a beautiful landscape (natural and human) to explore!

Photo credit SPOT tracker screenshot

# Episode 5

*Posted on March 11, 2015*

Magical moments in Nashville, and my first ever "tagging" just happens to be on a Cadillac! From covered wooden bridges in Georgia to snow covered mountain roads in northern Arizona. I hope you enjoy. https://youtu.be/_DQx51bJ9yY

# Taste of Dakar

*Posted on March 16, 2015*

So I was right off the strip in a hotel of Las Vegas and got a call that I should come out into the deserts of Pahrump, NV! I grabbed the bike rode through the Red Rock Canyon and off I went from a cozy hotel to sleeping in a car (I had left my camp kit at the hotel as at first I was just going to stay for the day – but after being at the event for a couple of hours I knew I would be staying)…and it was completely worth it!

Not just the stars in the sky and the beauty the nights hold out there but the group of people out at the Taste of Dakar were wonderful.

I did not do too much off-road riding but I did get to watch the Dakar podium holder – Jimmy Lewis teach an awesome skills class. He makes it look so easy and I loved the fact that if people would say, "well but my bike…" he would then hop on and ride their bike for the same uphill skill on the quarry to show that it is skill and can be done!

Sand dunes to cracked sand beds, dirt trails and winding valleys there was a bunch of eye candy for the ADV riders that came out. Amelia of course was the only Bonneville but was accepted and on opening night we shared the Right This Minute news feature that had just released and did a little chat with the group – which was a great intro and gave people a good starting point for conversation.

I met really neat riders -talked all things bikes and ADV travel, I got to have my first true jam session with my harmonica – it helps when you play with talented musicians as they make you sound good – like a good dance instructor. (Thank you Evan Firstman). Also met up with Brad Barker of Ride of Your Like and we taped a podcast that will air in a couple of months. (*not sure that it ever aired) I have to thank Fonse my friend who sent the invite my way, and Kurt who helped me find my way when I arrived. It was a great event and good group of people – will have to join Jeremy and crew at one of their events in the future for some true Taste of Dakar riding! (for more information visit http://www.altrider.com)

# The Bill Factor

*Posted on March 27, 2015*

I was getting new AVON tires and was quite excited! I called up Bill and Susan Dragoo and asked if I could send them to their house and were they up for a visit – I was invited in and Bill even let me know that he had a shop I could use as well.

When I arrived my ETD (estimated time of departure) had changed from just a couple days to being able to spend 5 days with the Dragoo's! It turned out to be not just an amazing visit with them both but much needed love to Amelia as well.

Our days started out with tea and bananas and then off to the gym for about an hour (except one day Susan took me on a beautiful trail run through Sutton

Wilderness, we opted out of indoor treadmill time).
Then we would return home and have a great nutrient
packed breakfast and Bill and I would head into the
shop to work on Amelia....

Well here is the "Bill factor" – and he is so patient to
allow the extra work and take the time to really work
through it all with me! We started off with the idea of
just doing tires and oil change– then with Bill's keen eye
Amelia showed her true colors as she knew she was in
good hands...what started as a one day quick job –
turned into a call to Truimph America and a gracious
overnight box containing the much needed steering
head components to replace the bearings to fix a detent,
rear rotor, new brake pads, and all the lock tight bolts
for the rotor (big thank you to Triumph North America
for the support and Todd!)

Then it came time to do the work I had planned –
putting on the new AVON tires! I am grateful to Craig
from Freedom Cycles in Las Vegas as he had nothing but
great things to say about the quality – I am definitely
excited to put the rubber to the road and test them out!
I was also able to head out to Oklahoma City and visit
with a new Triumph certified Dealer and thank you to
them for the support of oil and filter – AC the owner is a
very kind guy!

So the "Bill factor" taught me lots about Amelia and
caught so much that needed to be done, what is the "Bill
factor" well to me the -"Bill Factor" is an open heart,
genuine spirit and all around wonderful person and the
"Bill factor" is in both Susan and Bill – amazing hearts! I
have been blessed to spend a week with such souls!
From bike work to gym time, to evening wrap up in
relaxation watching a TV program with wine, to the
meals and the gun range- it was a wonderful time!

DANELL LYNN

# Where do you go...

Working on my article for 2 Wheeled Wanderlust the Magazine for the Spring / Summer issue out in May and I couldn't help but find myself thinking...

Where do I go from here...

Not in the literal sense of where – location, but when you feel completely vulnerable and open, and at the most centered that you have felt in years...where then do you go?

I am into my 7th month and have fun visits to dealerships lined up, new National Parks to visit and so many people yet to meet and places to see – it all just seems-well-ideal! And when you realize that the decisions you made 2 years ago to take this journey was the right choice in so many different ways...it is wonderful and odd at the same time because I have now passed through the halfway point. I am half way into my trip (glass half full) or over half way done (glass half empty)!

I have grown and seen some changes in myself in my time on the road, and have come far with expanding the social shell a little and let wonderful experiences in that I otherwise would have never chanced!

I have missed friends engagements, babies births / adoptions, and yet those friends are encouraging and supportive. It is beautiful to know especially growing up as a military dependent (home and friends changed every 2 or 3 years) now I have established a set of friends that will be with me for the rest of my life – they were here before I left on my journey and a new road family that has been growing – there will definitely be new additions to the family Christmas Letter I send out each year!

DANELL LYNN

## April 2015

### Inspirational Amelia
*April 17, 2015 // 0 Comments*

I have had a respect and admiration for Amelia Earhart for many years, and when going off on adventure for a year ( statements of correlation from my great-aunt) on my [...]

### So what's a Million Years
*April 16, 2015 // 2 Comments*

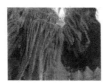

It did not occur overnight and truly makes one reflect on the famous saying, "a journey of a thousands miles begins with one step" – it may have taken a [...]

### Dixie Stampede
*April 14, 2015 // 0 Comments*

While in Branson, MO I took in a show ! I arrived on a Sunday – there was not a full variety of shows but it worked out as I have been visiting many National Park and [...]

### Restful get-a-way
*April 14, 2015 // 0 Comments*

The rain started as just a simple spring shower and became a cold, continuous drip! It was interesting to cross from Missouri and look right at the gray sky I was heading [...]

### Road Cheffing
*April 9, 2015 // 1 Comment*

Many people have asked how I eat on the road if I do not go out everyday...the simple answer – the same way I ate while living in a home – I take the time to [...]

## Spring Break
*April 8, 2015 // 0 Comments*

When one first thinks about "Spring Break" adventures – the mind usually does not go on a trip with your parents. But that is exactly what made it into my [...]

## The Royal Gorge
*April 1, 2015 // 2 Comments*

In 2013 I was on another motorcycle trip – a summer ride with mom and dad to the four corners and farther up into Colorado. We had planned at that time to ride over [...]

# The Royal Gorge

*Posted on April 1, 2015*

In 2013 I was on another motorcycle trip – a summer ride with mom and dad to the four corners and farther up into Colorado. We had planned at that time to ride over America's highest suspension bridge – the fires in Colorado that season made different plans.

Much of our route we had to leave as just a hopeful return to one day – we actually road into evacuation towns and ultimately had to turn around and head back south – we called that our end to Colorado for the 2013 ride.

Now 2 1/2 years later while out on my year-long journey mom and dad met up with me for a spring break ride and we took on Colorado again – and had an amazing time. And YES we got to ride the Royal Gorge bridge this time, what an amazing sight!

When it was constructed in 1929 it was captivating to the world and has stayed unique to that claim – still today bringing visitors from all over the world. During the 2013 fire it did survive just having 100 boards that needed to be replaced (other parts of the park / area were not as lucky but much has been rebuilt and on its way to flourishing again).

The bridge hangs over a beautifully laid out gorge of nature's design at an elevation of 6,700 feet and almost 1,000 feet above the Arkansas River – it is not for the faint of heart! But with pride I say that my father who struggles with heights rode his bike over – and even if he did not look down, he rode the 1200 ft length from one end to the other – and back again!

A definite site to see when in Colorado, the natural elements and man-made engineered phenomenon will captivate you for sure!

# Spring Break

*Posted on April 8, 2015*

When one first thinks about "Spring Break" adventures – the mind usually does not go on a trip with your parents. But that is exactly what made it into my calendar!

I took off from Las Vegas, Nevada and mom and dad left from Tucson, AZ – we met in Colorado for 5 days of riding and adventuring. After a long day of riding one of our stops was at *Joyful Journey's* for a stay in a Yurt! Glamping Colorado style! And it was a natural hot springs so evening and morning dips were required. (The cover picture for this post, " Clothing Required" is from this hot springs).

We rode the Million Dollar Highway with snow packed sides, even made a stop for a snow angel and snow man all while dressed in our moto-gear. As it needed to be we took a photo stop while riding by an active ski slope.

It felt amazing to ride through those mountains – the roads were perfect, as were the days – with only the need for heated gear a few times usually near the evenings.

We had a nice loop in Colorado and made it up to the Royal Gorge Bridge and then down to the Great Sand Dunes National Park before heading into New Mexico on route to Santa Fe. The Dunes are a sight for sure and just odd – surrounded by powerful mountains sits these hills of sand ever-changing in the winds.

We would have two days together in Santa Fe which of course we kicked off in true spring break fashion! After arriving to our hotel, through some rain, we began to hang our jackets and CRACK-BAM! There goes the wall shelf and dad standing there catching the helmets, holding the shelf...so it may not have been a party that trashed our hotel. When they came in to fix it and drilled it right back into drywall with no anchors and not into studs, we laughed and asked for an extra ironing board – that is where we hung our gear this time!

It is a cherished spring break not soon to be forgotten!

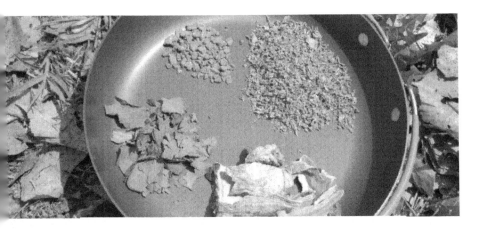

# Road Cheffing

*Posted on April 9, 2015*

Many people have asked how I eat on the road if I do
not go out every day...the simple answer – the same
way I ate while living in a home. I take the time to cook
it. I am also a vegetarian and there are places along the
road that are quite hard to find sustenance  meals. Yes
there is always a salad or mashed potatoes but without
a protein somewhere in there – it will be burned
through within the hour and I would be hungry again. (I
do also go out in towns when visiting friends or to eat
some local foods which is great fun as well). The trip is a
healthy blend of eating out and camp cooking, and the
home cooked meals I receive sometimes while out
traveling!

Much of this trip is "old-school" – I am traveling with no
GPS just maps, I have a "dumb-phone" and no
connection to internet unless in a hotspot, I am cooking

my meals as I go, and I saved for 2 years before I headed out! So it seems natural to me that I would want to also cook while camping!

I come by my love of cooking honestly as my mother and grandmother are amazing cooks and it has become part of my trip for them to travel with me – not literal but in my panniers!

I have an entire pannier dedicated to food – not much for cooking just a pot and pan, collapsible bowl and cup, and a multi-use set of utensils. Beyond that I give myself two small / medium (depending on the brand you buy) stuff sacks that I carry dehydrated food in. I buy fresh while out on the road – I prefer farmers stands and markets but when they aren't around I will hit a grocery time and again. My grandmother dehydrated many things for me to have variety, although I always have my staple of beans and rice if I need to whip up a quick meal. The benefit of grandmas foods is there are no additives and no salts (the kind you purchase is good for short trips but for a year it becomes unhealthy rather fast). I also have seasoning packs from mom and of course garlic olive oil and balsamic, and even some hand-picked mushrooms dehydrated down from my aunt and uncle!

It will never be said about me, "she eats like a bird" I have always been a big eater and like food very much (the process and the eating of it) so being on the road with the support of family helping to send meal restocking is just wonderful.

So yes I cook on the road in a jet boil pot and pan, and from that you can make a lot. There are many books out there for camp cooking and even if you feel it is too much to carry there are great ones out there for  bicycle cooking and they have even less space than I do :)! I do carry protein bars for that mid-day pick me up while out there riding!

My favorite snack on the road is portabella mushroom jerky – just pick your favorite spice cut your slices and dehydrate – I used to make this back home as well...so tasty...although it takes a lot to make a little bag and if you are like me – you will eat this quickly! Cheers to good eating out there on the road – and may it treat you well!

# Restful get-a-way

*Posted on April 14, 2015*

The rain started as just a simple spring shower and became a cold, continuous drip! It was interesting to cross from Missouri and look right at the gray sky I was heading toward in Arkansas!

I was on a mission, I had a room for the night at the Hyatt Place in Rogers, AR and could not have asked for a better location! I got to see some sights as I rode in and one made my chill feel a little less as I rode through Pea Ridge Battlefield – National Military Park! I read through accounts from the soldiers of their fingers being so cold that they could not even load their pistols – not even to save their lives! I definitely was not that cold, and the weather today was in the 60's not sub-zero temps of December 1862! It was a very neat site and determined to drive through the battlefield even in the rain, made for a unique viewing as I only saw one other car the entire 7 mile loop!

Then I heard the hotel was ready, and man was I! I got in and took off my rain suit outside so as not to completely soak the lobby. Amelia got front row parking under the awning and off I went to the 5th floor!

A quick order from their 24 hour food gallery and then a warm bath! I have always been a lover of the rain and storms, but I must say I enjoy them so much more with a warm cup of coffee and looking out my fifth floor window into the rolling hills in the hazy distance than riding through it on tarmac.

Complete with work desk, living area and bedroom – I was completely set and ready to work! Thank you Hyatt Place Rogers, AR for such a  great stay and the staff were very kind as well! Thank greatly Janet Mason it was lovely.

# Dixie Stampede

*Posted on April 14, 2015*

While in Branson, MO I took in a show ! I arrived on a Sunday – there was not a full variety of shows but it worked out as I have been visiting many National Park and National Historic sites that relate to Americas past – so to attend the Dixie Stampede was fitting actually.

It was fun to arrive into Branson, my initial plan was to camp at the state park lake...that is until I saw all the signs filled with much to do in the city. I decided it would be a good night for a hotel stay and maybe a show.

I was talking with my folks and learned my grandmother Edith use to love Branson and taking in the shows! I did not know that while on trek to the city but once I did I felt like she was with me for my evening and my dinner show!

From wagon races to settlers and Native tales, there were horses and buffalo and even pig and chicken races! With a four course meal and cheers, it is an interesting event fun for family or solo!

It was definitely a packed show that left me a little teary eyed at the end!

The finale was a salute of Red, White and Blue. 10 horses and riders dressed in American colors and waving America flags as Dolly Parton (not in person but on the big screen) sang songs of freedom – "Color Me America"! The crowd stood and I could not help but feel my country pride boiling and the honor and gift I have to be able to do an adventure of this sorts! I have traveled to many countries and in many areas that women do not have the rights they have here – I am humbled, and honored to be the daughter and sister of military men who helped give the freedoms I have to be on a trip like this! Thank you – cheers to the show for bringing this up in me!

(don't forget to follow / like the Facebook page and see more updates and pictures through-out the journey – http://www.facebook.com/blacktie2blacktop )

# So what's a
# Million Years

*Posted on April 16, 2015*

It did not occur overnight and truly makes one reflect on the famous saying, "a journey of a thousand miles begins with one step" It may have taken a million years but the Ozark Uplift created mountains, then the rains eroded the surface, then rivers and streams created even deeper crevices that joined with rain water between the layers of limestone to create these amazing caverns throughout Missouri!

There are over 6,000 caves in the Missouri Ozarks, Bridal Cave is just one that I was able to visit and I had moments where I just held my mouth open in awe at the wave-like ripples in the stone! It was stunning!  In Camdenton, MO I rode to the caves before I stopped at the Lake of the Ozarks State Park for some camping. To go from the beauty of the underworld to the calmness of the lakes above is such a pure and calming experience!

And if you are married and would like to renew your vows – next Feb. 14, 2016 you can go to Bridal Cave for free, renew your vows, and get a goodie bag and pass for free lifetime entrance to the cave! They are called Bridal Cave and have held over 3000 weddings inside even on the day I visited after the tour and coming out there was the bridal party and guest ready to enter for the ceremony.

# Inspirational Amelia

*Posted on April 17, 2015*

I have had a respect and admiration for Amelia Earhart for many years, and when going off on adventure for a year (statements of common elements from my great-aunt) on my Triumph Bonneville I named her Amelia!

Now 7 months in we have had some pretty fantastic adventures filled with ups and downs, great weather and scary weather, and so much in between!

The power of historical figures in their ability to inspire is one of the greatest gift in literacy! I love that I have been able to read about so many women and men in history that I can look up at and think – yeah let's do it!

While at the end of my days in Kansas I was able to head north out of Kansas City into Atchison and visit the Birthplace home of Amelia Earhart! Which the town is a bit magical with stunning historic homes and beautiful brick streets, with rolling hills and greenery ..."Toto am I still in Kansas?"

I was lucky to be there with no other visitors. Just me and the women running the home (who was in her 70's), we chatted and I got to hear stories that had been shared with her from Amelia's sister and stories from other family members. It was a unique and special time and I think that she could see my true admiration for Amelia Earhart and so she spent a good half hour in the downstairs with me explaining much of the home and stories!

Even the bookshelves that hold original copies of adventure stories Mrs. Earhart read as a child, it was great to see similar titles that had inspired adventure when I too was a child – so many years apart but literature led to the same desire to see more and live more this was alive within us both!

See more pictures from my time here in the Kansas folder -http://bt2bt.smugmug.com/KS/

DANELL LYNN

### Winterized Spring – Overland Expo
*May 21, 2015 // 0 Comments*

Right now I am sitting at the base of Zion mountains camping by the river and watching hummingbirds play and deer nibble on fresh spring berries! This after an amazing 4 days [...]

### Diner Revival – Food Network Volunteering
*May 20, 2015 // 0 Comments*

While I was in Norman, Oklahoma I had the opportunity to work as a volunteer on the new Food Network show American Diner Revival. The crew was a wonderful blend of hard [...]

### Episode 6 – Month 6
*May 14, 2015 // 3 Comments*

Over half a year completed...see the new episode from Month 6! [...]

### Soundtrack of life
*May 9, 2015 // 2 Comments*

There are so many things we can learn through music. It has been a part of human nature for as long as we were able to pick up objects with our hands! I think music creates [...]

### Experience
*May 3, 2015 // 3 Comments*

Wildness of exhaustion. I feel so alive out in nature and traveling the nation with birds flying above me and around me...and at times I feel in flight myself! The [...]

# Experience

*Posted on May 3, 2015*

Wildness of exhaustion. I feel so alive out in nature and traveling the nation with birds flying above me and around me...and at times I feel in flight myself! The camping, the miles, the sun, the fresh air...it is easy to get lost within the beauty of the wild and then it will hit – the catch up of exhaustion!

This trip is amazing in so many ways and it always lets me know when I need to rest – sometimes it is after a full week of hard riding, sometimes just 4 days, but when the body speaks on a journey of this length I have learned to listen. I have learned that it is okay to take in rest, a break is needed and it is okay to slow-down. From this serial entrepreneur and workaholic that is a big lesson learned. I am blessed to have a trip like this be my teacher and the life lessons are vast and continue to teach me! 8 months in and I am more open, more calm, and more clear on what holds importance to me!

Although I have multiple days where I don't speak much to others – I see more in people as I take the time to really experience them when I am meeting new individuals. I really wanted to journal at a great campsite in Indiana-but the universe had other plans-my solitude was put on hold by the bright light of children. I sat at my picnic table and worked on building my camp fire when I looked up at a little girl who was screaming for her nana — her sister (maybe 5 yrs old) had just crashed her training-wheeled bicycle and was laying under it...about to cry...I glanced around and could not just watch this child...she was only 15 feet from me. So I ran over – picked the bike up while untwisting her leg -chatting the entire time with her about how brave she was, and how we sometimes fall...and as she stood up – tearless- we did a big high-five and that was it! For the next 4 hours, with their nana's approval, I had 2 young ladies (maybe 5 and 7) hanging out at my picnic table. We read books, talked about camping, baby-dolls, and about where I live.

It is different to explain a trip like mine to a child. The older of the two asked me:

"Where do you live?"
A:- I live on the road, on my bike and in this tent.

"But where do you live, where is your house?"
A"-I don't have one, I sold everything I did not want and put my keepsakes into storage, I am hoping to find a place to call home while out on the road.

"But where is your husband?"
A:- I don't have one of those either.

She just stared at me with an odd look and a pause, then she said, "oh" and with that we were on to talking about bigger things like bicycle riding and preschool activities!

The simple pleasures are more abundant on this journey and I hope that is a lesson that sticks with me for years to come! And allowing myself the time to simply sit or rest...maybe I will take a rest now – cheers to naps.

Photo credit - Triumph North America

# Soundtrack of life

*Posted on May 9, 2015*

There are so many things we can learn through music, it has been a part of human nature for as long as we were able to pick up objects with our hands!

I think music creates the soundtrack to our lives and I love having mine circling through my helmet as I ride! People often wonder if I have completely silent helmet time and contemplation...and yes maybe only 10% of the time though. Part of my daily prep in putting my helmet on is preparing my music! I think music can often guide you into those depths of contemplation...and man do I get those out on the open road for hours!

I have always loved varied – in so many aspects of living – but definitely in music. I do not just listen to one type on the road or in my stationary life, I love quite a bit, as long as it moves me or plays to an emotion then it is the right music!

Often it will fade into the background as my thoughts or ideas run rampant, but you might also catch me dancing as I ride, it is just something that I cannot control! Good music moves the soul and the body so why fight it.

On the road I am trying to learn Harmonica and a Lakota Flute both are going well, although I mostly spend my camping time learning the flute now as it blends so well with the nature and birds around me! I like the Harmonica for jam sessions with musicians as they help guide me and make my limited skills sound good!

I have been refreshed of my love of live music and also to playing music on this trip...for many years I had stopped – not sure why exactly I guess the age-old reasoning of life got busy. As a child I played the piano, as a teen I took a year of guitar... then when I went off to college and university I just stopped! One thing is for sure – wherever I end up after this journey – learning a new instrument or igniting old loves will be a part of my life!

# Episode 6 – Month 6

*Posted on May 14, 2015*

Over half a year completed...see the new episode from Month 6!

https://youtu.be/rio0xjjPiE4

# Diner Revival – Food Network Volunteering

*Posted on May 20, 2015*

While I was in Norman, Oklahoma I had the opportunity to work as a volunteer on the new Food Network show American Diner Revival. The crew was a wonderful blend of hard workers and people on a mission to help revive and give new life to classic diners. I was honored to be a part of the renovation.

I got to work on a wide variety of projects in the two days with the show...loved what they did with reclaimed wood design around the bar...just by use of old pallets cut down and layers in a unique clean line design.

From staining to sealing and cutting to carrying...there was never a dull moment on set of the new show featuring hosts Ty Pennington and Amanda Freitag blending their two passions beautifully of creative design and culinary expressions with Barrett Washburne -btw one of the most gentle souls I have met in a long time – and fantastic Food Stylist!

Check out the show and enjoy the season -the show premiers Friday, May 22 at 10:30 / 9:30c. There are 6 episodes where towns come together to revive old loves and surprise the owners!

See more of my behind the scenes pics from the work days: http://bt2bt.smugmug.com/Diner-Revival-Food-Network/i-kkpNk4m

# Winterized Spring – Overland Expo

*Posted on May 21, 2015*

Right now I am sitting at the base of Zion mountains camping by the river and watching hummingbirds play and deer nibble on fresh spring berries! This after an amazing 4 days at the Overland Expo West.

The weather was calling for it, out running tornadoes and braving T-storms – the only way to make it from the east back west for what would turn out to be an adventure in weather all it's own!

Arriving to a beautiful day, soon the clouds began to roll in and created a mud puddle for the weekend. We had wind, snow, rain and weird gusts of all three...and yet in true Overland fashion it was amazing!

I was part of the Author group tent again this year and sold out of the Young Readers edition – Purposeful Wanderings and almost sold out of Philanthropic Wanderlust (was quite pleased considering you had to cross a lake of rain water to get to our tent- our adventure readers braved it!)

This year was my talk in the main theater on my first 8 months of my Black Tie 2 Black Top journey. I had a few AT issues but once resolved I talked to a packed house! I felt so honored to be able to share my story and to have so many people interested. The talk about my journey was set up more as an inspirational lecture on getting out the comfort zone living and taking on that unconventional life! After my presentation people kept coming up to me with warm regards and kind words! It was wonderful!!

I also did a demo on packing up the medium sized bike and my choice for the adventure a Triumph Bonneville decked out in Giant Loop Moto bags. The group had great questions on things from the bike mechanics, to the type of under gear and outer gear (REV'IT) that I use on this journey.

For the past 3 years I have been a part of the panel on philanthropy and Doing Good as you Go and this year was great again! I find that even in a large crowd...it is that one person you reach that is changing their lives by changing the lives of others – what inspiration at this event.

It was also an amazing weekend for networking, growth and new kit. I am happy to have the new Atlas Throttle lock now on Amelia for the ride, and no more crazy cords everywhere as I am rocking out with Sena for the ride! (and my month 9 and forward

will be captured with their cameras). I have also
received a beautiful jacket to wear when off the bike
(used as the commuter jacket in town on your bike it is
quite versatile ) the clean lines and elegant cut
of Aether gear is stunning – now when walking the
cities I will do so in style and not just in my under-layer
heated gear jacket!

So excited for all the new future endeavors that OX held
the doors open for and you can expect some great
updates within the next month as things go official.

(**this is when I signed on as the female rider for
Expedition Electric – we rode electric motorbikes from
the Arctic Circle, Alaska and into Canada – the plan was
for further...only time will tell. I was also invited to be
the female rider for a documentary with Brad Barker of
*The Ride of My Life* -to Cambodia – after a quick call to
Guinness World committee I was given a go-featured in
the next blog of this book!)

## June 2015

### Cycle Gear – Press
June 20, 2015 // 2 Comments

Breaking Boundaries and Records – For years – as a riding family – we have received Cycle Gear catalog...they have since created Cycle Gear catalog [...]

### SHE Rescue Home
June 15, 2015 // 1 Comment

We often forget inside the cush of life that there is so much pain and incomprehensible decisions being made. When I first was asked about coming on the Cambodian "The [...]

### Cambodia and Her People
June 15, 2015 // 0 Comments

There is an underlying spirituality here for sure. The calm that washes over you as you take in the environment, the people and even the technical riding...there is a [...]

### Cambodia-Joining the "Ride of My Life" –
June 6, 2015 // 1 Comment

At Overland Expo just a few short weeks back I was invited by Brad Barker of The Ride of My Life to join their team about to depart for an amazing Cambodia Adventure. I was [...]

# Cambodia-Joining the "Ride of My Life" –

*Posted on June 6, 2015*

At Overland Expo just a few short weeks back I was invited by Brad Barker of *The Ride of My Life* to join their team about to depart for an amazing Cambodian Adventure.

I was not able to get the post out pre-departure...but it works out because now I am writing you from Cambodia! I will be in country about 9 days and experiencing as much as possible. We will do a few days as "tuk-tuk" riding tourist around Siem Reap and to Angkor Wat and then we will get our Yamaha 250 dirt bikes for some back road adventuring through Cambodia. Once we are good and muddy and exhausted we will arrive in Phenom Penh and provide 22 quilts and 2 baby quilts from my foundation *Threading Hope* to the *SHE rescue House* (for more on this visit http://www.ThreadingHope.com)

So for now cheers to adventure...and yes this break to ride Cambodia is approved and within the guidelines of Guinness World Record so when I return I will pick BT2BT ride back up and continue on my year journey through all 50 states and Canada...but you know it is not too bad of a reason to pause!

Stay the most up to date on all the adventure through my Black Tie 2 Black Top Facebook and my Danell Lynn Twitter and Instagram pages!

# Cambodia and Her People

*Posted on June 15, 2015*

There is an underlying spirituality here for sure. The calm that washes over you as you take in the environment, the people and even the technical riding...there is a spirit that resides within this beautiful country.

I felt moved in the presence of children along the Mekong River that played and laughed although their home was a shack - their lives were unbelievably rich! The children in Cambodia reached deep within me as the young often can...they still have the innocence and far enough removed from the late 1970's Khmer Rouge and Civil War that followed...they are just in love with life and it is contagious.

This trip was filled with improved riding skills and new challenges that I overcame on the bike. I leave with a new dirt confidence and will hear my team in my ear when I hit that hard patch of soft sand – "just let it dance, throttle up...." They were great supporters and teachers I could not have had a better group and my sweep guide – Dave from Cambodia was amazing and really took time to teach me the skills that created a wonderful off-road journey.

I will be back to Cambodia one day – the country will stick with me for a while and on our second to last day in country we walked along the killing fields and sadly that too will stick with me – as it had just rained so many bones had risen to the surface – it is heart wrenching sometimes what humanity does to its own kind. Every time I visit or read about atrocities like this ... I just truly cannot understand how one person does this to another...and yet the country smiles and her people hold deep hopes and joy even though the darkness was not much more than 30 years ago.

Cambodia has my heart – she has moved me and I have fallen in love with the joy and spirit that resides here. It has been an amazing journey and so honored that The Ride of My Life let me be a part of the documentary journey here! (The film should release in the next 6 months)

# SHE Rescue Home

*Posted on June 15, 2015*

We often forget inside the cush of life that there is so much pain and incomprehensible decisions being made.

When I first was asked about coming on the Cambodian *The Ride of My Life* expedition I immediately wondered how can Threading Hope be of use while there. I had read a couple of books and watched a few documentaries over the years on the problems of human trafficking little girls and wanted our quilts to somehow go to these children.

With research I found the SHE Rescue Home and began to correspond with the Phenom Penh program. The work that they are doing is moving to say the least and so very powerful. While at the same time – for me – creating an internal unease and disgust with humanity – as many of the young girls trafficked are as little as 6 years old and sold for the evening to international pedophiles that come to this underground network specifically for that reason.

It is heart wrenching but because of people like those in this group there is hope at least for some of these girls to find a new path. The saddest thing is many of the children are sold into these rings by their parents as a way to pay off debts.

SHE Rescue Home staff member David welcomed us into the center to meet with him and learn more of the program. We provided them 22 quilts and 2 baby quilts to their request for the girls at the home and the 2 babies born to rescued girls in their care.

He was very thankful and let us know that the girls would find much joy in the quilts and that many only come into the facility with just the one set of clothes they are wearing...and now they will each have their very own quilt hand-made with love from quilt donations around the nation. So humbled to be a part of the healing even at a distance. Thank you SHE Rescue Home for all you do!

(**Threading Hope has been supporting children and families in need for over 8 years – do you know a quilter that would like to donate – find us at www.ThreadingHope.com)

**-Bonus not a blog but a needed memory to mention here** It amazes me the way that life works, after visiting the She Rescue House and then the Killing Fields, the flight home was somber to say the least.

We did not speak much but a we got ready to depart our airport lounge in Shanghai – life would complete the circle. I was able to sit with the Dalai Lama and discuss Threading Hope-the deliveries, the visit to the Killing Fields…and as he held my hand he reminded me that not all people are good, although we try our best.

It was magical and a truly inspirational way to end the trip that had many emotions twisted within me – after our meeting I felt weightless and calm as he reminded me of our heart and that deep down humanity is good.

Cherished moment for sure, wish my camera battery had not died – this was taken on a phone – but captured for the mental memories when I am old – or now when I need reminded!

**Breaking Boundaries—and Records**

Last September, Danell Lynn set out to ride through all 50 states and Canada by motorcycle. On a trip she's dubbed "1 Woman, 1 Bike, 1 Year," Lynn is attempting to break the Guinness World Record of "longest journey by motorcycle in a single country," which she hopes to achieve by riding her Triumph Bonneville through the 48 contiguous United States. Then she'll continue the slog on to Hawaii, Alaska and Canada. As of May 14, Lynn's trip has already covered 27 states and more than 30,000 miles. (The most recent Guinness World Record in this category was set in 2014, a 23,761-mile run.) See more of Lynn's blog at danelllynn.wordpress.com.

# Cycle Gear – Press

*Posted on June 20, 2015*

Breaking Boundaries and Records –

For years – as a riding family – we have received Cycle Gear catalog...they have since created *Cycle Gear catalog & Magazine* – and the first issue out this July has a feature about Amelia and my journey! Honored to have a feature in the catalog that we have gotten in our mailbox so many times before!!

You can pick up the new issue out now at your Cycle Gear stores nearest you. I believe I am on page 8!

DANELL LYNN

## July 2015

### Fun in Foods
*July 29, 2015 // 2 Comments*

I have talked about my talented grandmother before and as the adventure continues it has been fun to receive my refills of dehydrated foods on the road. Grams has been [...]

### Month 7 – Episode 7 – webisode
*July 27, 2015 // 3 Comments*

Take a journey with me into month 7 on my year long adventure. Captured in a short webisode to hightlight the [...]

### This Thing Called LIFE – article published
*July 26, 2015 // 0 Comments*

OutdoorX4 magazine has published one of my articles on the first part of my journey! Check it out in Issue 9. http://www.OutdoorX4.com The magazine features a bunch of [...]

### Glaciation and ...
*July 25, 2015 // 3 Comments*

With the natural "old-growth forests, wind-swept prairies, ancient glaciers, and deep lakes" it is no wonder they consider this a world in itself. The ride [...]

### Simplicity on the Road
*July 23, 2015 // 4 Comments*

It is amazing to me what you can pack your life down into...and I thought I went small when I put all my belongings into a 10×7' storage shed...that was [...]

## Great Falls KOA- Fall in Love...

*July 12, 2015 // 2 Comments*

Surrounded by a field of trees lies the lovely campground of Great Falls KOA. Started with flat lands of Montana in the 1970's they have planted and maintained the [...]

## Yellowstone National Park

*July 10, 2015 // 7 Comments*

There are so many words that could be used to describe this majestic place – but I think that it creates the best visual and the scenes that are burned into my mind to [...]

# Yellowstone National Park

*Posted on July 10, 2015*

There are so many words that could be used to describe this majestic place – but I think that it creates the best visual and the scenes that are burned into my mind to just simply say – Yellowstone is like a fine art painting!

I have seen her landscapes painted over the years with the rolling hills and dense forests and just thought that artists took a liberty to add in the depth of colors – but no it IS like a painting and just as captivating.

I stayed for 3 days in Lewis Lake campground near the south entrance of the park! A great location right on the lake and nestled in the forest. It is one of the more primitive sites but does have toilets and also important – individual bear boxes for all your goodies. Not only do you feel more "Yellowstone" here it is only $15 a night. And if you come in summer when the camp host Larry is on duty – give a big hello to him from me – and be sure to chat with him (this man has years of wonderful stories from Yellowstone).

The natural elements kept me in awe, although it was the wildlife that got my heart beating! I was lucky enough to see a young male moose, a mother grizzly bear and two cubs, bison galore (but one very close up – was a little nerve wrecking) and herds of elk! I could not have asked for a more filled trip!

And the geysers – well not only did I watch front row for Old Faithful but that days crowd was lucky to also see Bee Hive erupt just minutes after. Bee Hive lasts longer, shoots higher and only goes off 1 or 2 times a day!

Yellowstone was an adventure for sure although I could have used more days to see it all – 3 days just does not cover it. As the World's First National Park it sure does live up to all the hype and the memories I had from the visit when I was just in kindergarten almost 30 years ago! Just stunning!

# Great Falls KOA- Fall in Love...

Posted on July 12, 2015

Surrounded by a field of trees lies the lovely campground of Great Falls KOA. Started with flat lands of Montana in the 1970's they have planted and maintained the beautiful site you will now see today.

Unique to others in its home feeling offerings with a kamp kitchen (where you can get a 2 eggs, hash-browns and toast with coffee for just $5.00) and this summer nightly has blue grass and folk inspired live music, not to mention it also has large RV sites, Kamp Cabins (which I enjoyed for two nights) a pool (more of a mini-water park), wifi and loads of stuff for kids to keep busy!

The staff was right away welcoming and excited to be a part of my cross-country journey! The Kamp Kabins if you don't know are great little writing houses (this is how I see them – a little Walden on the road) with a full size bed and a bunk bed with a desk and AC (you may think for Montana...but it is unseasonably warm and I was very grateful for AC)!

Another unique quality to this particular KOA is that it has free firewood and right outside my cabin was a fire pit and picnic table nestled under great trees and although in a commercial camp ground – it felt very private and spacious! A lovely facility and location.

Not too far for my ride out tomorrow to make it to Glacier National Park in the north-western part of the state. A great stay and great staff – I can honestly recommend a stay over at the Great Falls KOA – call ahead for reservations to guarantee your space as word about this gem gets out!

# Simplicity on the Road

*Posted on July 23, 2015*

It is amazing to me what you can pack your life down into...and I thought I went small when I put all my belongings into a 10×7' storage shed...that was until I decided to live out of 3 bags for a year.

1 pannier is for food and my kitchen, 1 is for my clothing allowance (that is except the outer REV'IT gear I ride in), my larger bag is my home- all my inside gear for my tent and putting together my bedroom each night (you can see more on all my bags – Giant Loop, my tent – LoneRider, Kit and gear and my riding gear – REV'IT on the Bike & Kit page on my website).

There are days that I still feel like I carry too much, and yet when I really look at what I have simplified my life to, for this year on the road, it amazes me how little we really need.

And yet in such a simplified and planned organization on the road – this week I somehow lost my wrench for my rear axle bolt so that I could tighten my chain...where on earth it could have gone – no idea (so guess it would have to be the first lost object on the road...actually the second as I did lose my hair wrap in high winds. It pulled and blew right out the helmet just last month) This also does not count the Jetboil lid that was stolen by Virginia mountain rats! (literally rats). But in the grand scheme of 10 months on the road, not too bad I think.

Although I know returning to a "typical" lifestyle will have more needs / wants, I know I will live with less. Before this trip I was embracing the beauty of less and now I will do so with so much more insight into to what it is that I really need! It will be exciting to go back through all those tubs in my 10×7' and wonder what I was thinking when I paid to store some of this "stuff"!

(The picture used for this post is from my prep days pre-departure, I have since pared down even more while out on the road)

(*Soon after this trip I took a job in the Grand Canyon on Havasupai Indian Reservation and stayed in a small apartment for 6 months. After that I joined Expedition Electric and lived on the road or a few more months before returning to Tucson and beginning the build of my "tiny house" **)

# Glaciation and ...

*Posted on July 25, 2015*

With the natural "old-growth forests, wind-swept prairies, ancient glaciers, and deep lakes" it is no wonder they consider this a world in itself. The ride through the park is on the famed -"Going to the Sun" road that will take you either west to east or east to west – the choice is yours.

For a world in itself it sure opened the doors wide to how small a world we are all riding. During my time in Yellowstone I met fellow Triumph rider – Rob and his family in a parking lot...and they were also headed to Glacier (put that with 5 campgrounds and all full what were the odds that we met up again just one row apart once I finally found a site).

The smallness continued as I rode into the last campground in hopes for an open site as they were all full... and for the last two campgrounds I was circling within the with another Bonneville and BMW rider. So when I stopped to ask the camp host if there was anything left – well the universe stepped in again.

There were a couple other people waiting to talk with her and my two fellow camp hopefuls parked nearby when a man walked up and stated that he had paid for a site and did not need it anymore! Before the sentence was out of his mouth I glanced at my other two riders and asked the man – can we buy it from you! Thus the family – community site began. Josh, Cody and I all introduced ourselves and then rode off to site C-133 to set up camp.

After we got our site set up we were met by another rider – a woman on the road solo for two months...thus Valerie joined the family on site C-133. Then we were doing our dinners when a bicyclist rode up and asked if he could have a spot, thus Buddy became a part of the family.

Then I got a text from a fellow adv. world rider – Alex from Germany and he also became a part of our small world family. (Alex and I would be ride buddies the next day across Montana)!

Thank goodness they did not have rules to how many tents can set up on one site – because we sure filled it! I ended up extending a day and for day 2 it was just Josh, Cody, Alex and I. We did a small ride together into town for firewood, dinner and wine! We had a great community evening of riders and stories – the history of this area bringing people together as a meeting place sure continues. It was lovely.

# This Thing Called LIFE
# – article published

*Posted on July 26, 2015*

OutdoorX4 magazine has published one of my articles on the first part of my journey! Check it out in Issue 9. http://www.OutdoorX4.com

The magazine features a bunch of different adventure stories and articles – honored to be a contributing writer! Hope you enjoy. (you can subscribe via email and read it free or purchase a hard copy of the magazine!)

There will be a follow up article and adventures down the road as well. Great publishers.

*Posted on July 27, 2015*

Take a journey with me into month 7 on my year long adventure. Captured in a short webisode to hightlight the journey.

https://youtu.be/1-GShUfJtm0

# Fun in Foods

*Posted on July 29, 2015*

I have talked about my talented grandmother before and as the adventure continues it has been fun to receive my refills of dehydrated foods on the road.

Grams has been experimenting with what she can dehydrate and has made some great concoctions for me to create within my Jetboil or with a few fresh additions.

Pictured on this blog feature page is of Coconut bacon (a vegan delight) and makes some wonderful BLT's on the road. I have also made from her dehydrated foods – cheese pasta, tomatoes, roasted garlic, added a bit of olive oil and man – tasty!

For breakfast most of my days are packed with a hardy granola (did I mention that all grams foods are processed / preservative free...I know...I really do know how lucky I am). To the granola, that is already packed with goodness, I add some of her dehydrated apples, grapes or cherries, and a few tablespoons of Chia seeds to top it off!

The other night it was a little chilly in northern Minnesota so I was able to do a soup with her dehydrated corn and carrots. Adding to it a pinch of garlic salt, garlic powder and about a tablespoon of the minced onions she also sent.

There are so many options and so much that can be made, I have learned so many new camp ideas and my grandmother is to credit as well as for keeping me well feed! I worried about losing weight on such a long journey as this and she has made sure that I never feel hunger pains! So to Grandma Phyllis – thank you and much love your way – it is a joy to cook and consume your creations. Below is a picture of the creation of the BLT – all my snacks and meals come labeled and packed in zip-locks for ease of use and creates great meal organization.

## August 2015

### Falling Water
August 28, 2015 // 5 Comments

The irony of the day was not lost on me! Falling Water was my end destination and I rode through Thunderstorm downpours (so Falling Water) all day long. From 9am until 6pm I [...]

### Walden
August 19, 2015 // 3 Comments

"I learned this, at least, by my experiment: that if one advances confidently in the direction of his dreams, and endeavors to live the life which he has imagined, he will [...]

### Quechee – Pine Valley KOA
August 16, 2015 // 1 Comment

It was following me all day – this threatening dark gray cloud threatening to swallow me up in the storm! As I was passing through to make New Hampshire I came across [...]

### A Little Oddity with a Big Name
August 13, 2015 // 2 Comments

What drew me to Salem, New Hampshire was not what might first come to mind – but I wanted to venture through the grounds of America's Stonehenge. Not sure what I [...]

### Niagara Falls
August 10, 2015 // 1 Comment

It was the first of August, and do you know what that means? It was Niagara Falls Day! On this trip I have tried to start each day with a big stretch, and then smile at the [...]

# Niagara Falls

*Posted on August 10, 2015*

It was the first of August, and do you know what that means? It was Niagara Falls Day!

On this trip I have tried to start each day with a big stretch, and then smile at the world and say good morning! It is a lovely way to start the day – and if I knew the chaos of people I would soon encounter I may have said it twice!

First of all I had my days all messed up – I thought I was arriving on Friday! Nope it was Saturday and packed. Traffic was crazy on the roads and the footpaths. So what does a girl do when surround by the beauty of the falls and the personal bubble encroaching crowds...Ice Cream!

I got a double scoop and walked the grounds. It was perfect. Then I decided to take it all in from the water and bought a pass for the *Maid of the Mist* – the famous boat journey that takes travelers to the waters beneath the American and Horseshoe Falls.

*Maid of the Mist* is aptly titled as you must wear a rain poncho and still it gets you! It was a hot day so one could not help but smile as the powerful splashing mist drenched your face! Another thing I did not know that Niagara Falls State Park is America's oldest state park. So I have now been to the oldest State Park and the first National Park (Yellowstone), pretty cool!

# A Little Oddity with a Big Name

*Posted on August 13, 2015*

What drew me to Salem, New Hampshire was not what might first come to mind – but I wanted to venture through the grounds of America's Stonehenge.

Not sure what I expected as I had not researched it all nor seen pictures just a listing in red on my map to guide me! Now I spent 4 years in my youth in the United Kingdom and when I thought of Stonehenge...I did not picture at all what I was about to see.

Although it does not give you the sense of the famous namesake -this location opened in 1958 as "mystery hill caves" and that is a little more fitting... but due to the historical belief of what the site may have been used for they changed the name in 1982.

It is privately owned and is $12 (at the time of this writing) for entrance and you are given a very detailed map and can stroll through at your own pace. All specific sites are listed by number or letter and it corresponds to the map so it is easy to self-guide through this historic location.

It is not too large, but in its quickness it holds on to you with something special! Was enjoyable and they had alpaca which I swear smiled  at me...but that might be more my desire to have a cabin, a little farm and raise alpaca for yarn and knit my own socks...one day!

# Quechee – Pine Valley

Posted on August 16, 2015

It was following me all day – this dark gray cloud threatening to swallow me up in the storm!

As I was passing through to make New Hampshire I came across the Pine Valley KOA in the eastern corner of Vermont! Michael and Cindy Scruggs were very welcoming and provided a wonderful night's stay for me in one of the kamping cabins.

From outdoor movies, to pancake breakfast all on location and not to mention the close attractions. I rode over to the Quechee cheese and grocery and got all Vermont local meals for my dinner that night (and at just a mile down the road it was perfect- nearby).

I came here after my visit to the Marsh-Billings-Rockefeller NHP visit and just across in New Hampshire is another National Historic Park.

# Walden

*Posted on August 19, 2015*

*"I learned this, at least, by my experiment: that if one advances confidently in the direction of his dreams, and endeavors to live the life which he has imagined, he will meet with a success unexpected in common hours."*
— Henry David Thoreau, Walden: Or, Life in the Woods

Some locations on this trip are filled with motion and music – like Nashville, or Chicago and some locations are simply for quiet contemplation – this was Walden.

There is a fluidity in life that gets its balance in silence. Sometimes just sitting on the edge of a historic pond is a drug in itself for your mind.

I found much peace at Walden and even with the locals swimming and enjoying the beaches – many were camped out under the shade reading!

It was in this moment that I realized I don't see that enough anymore...reading... I rarely find people engrossed in books as I travel. Often at historic sites I will see youth on Facebook and completely disjointed from the location they are visiting and this is a bit sad to me.

I yearn for Walden some days, and can understand why Thoreau needed to have this! It still is special and has an air of joy and peace unlike other ponds I visit...is that real or an emotion I have created for it? I am not sure but the feeling in me was real and I enjoyed my sack lunch and hike through Walden pond! It was my joy and to that – thank you Mr. Thoreau!

# Falling Water

*Posted on August 28, 2015*

The irony of the day was not lost on me! Falling Water was my end destination and I rode through Thunderstorm downpours (so Falling Water) all day long. From 9am until 6pm I was in my rain suit with sporadic moments of suns delight!

But alas on to the creative genius that was Frank Lloyd Wright! I have wanted to see Falling Water since I was quite young, it has always captivated me in a way that I could not explain – until now!  After seeing it in person and being present in such a seamless blend of nature and art thorough architecture I understood my deeply held desire to view this work of art! It was magnificent.

Designed in 1935 it quickly became the calling card that got Frank Lloyd Wright over 400 more commissions for work (he was already in his 70s). Talk about true passion – he never stopped creating or designing – the only thing that stopped him was his death in his 90s.

It is the "only major Wright work to come into the public domain with its setting, original furnishings and artwork intact." In 1963 the Kaufmann family entrusted it to the Western Pennsylvania Conservancy!

It is truly a magical place, I would suggest signing up for the last tour of the day – that way when you head to the viewing area no other tourists will be in your photos!

DANELL LYNN

## September 2015

### Home ???
*September 22, 2015 // 1 Comment*

Are you ever coming home? I have a small handful of very good friends back in Arizona and from one of them in Phoenix -on a happy birthday text- she wrote -"Happy [...]

### *"Ponderance"
*September 20, 2015 // 4 Comments*

A few weeks ago I began pondering with the fastness of Alaska vanishing below me as I flew to Hawaii. I could not believe I was almost finishing my year on the road. It has [...]

### Amelia and Santa's Sleigh
*September 12, 2015 // 2 Comments*

A short story – ( this is a fun work of fiction inspired by a visit to the North Pole Alaska during my year long journey with my motorcycle – a Triumph Bonneville [...]

### To SHIP or not to SHIP
*September 11, 2015 // 1 Comment*

That was the question. I went back and forth and weeks of research on shipping my Amelia to Hawaii. I looked into planes and boats, and then also had to add weather into the [...]

## The Final Frontier

*September 10, 2015 // 4 Comments*

"hey world what do you say" great lyrics played as I recapped my time in Alaska! I could not have asked for a better 4 days in Alaska! i had a little rain on day [...]

## Denali National Park

*September 9, 2015 // 2 Comments*

As I left Fairbanks on highway 3 south I kept seeing this monster of a mountain in the distance. I thought could it be – am I seeing Mt. McKinley from here! I pulled [...]

# Denali National Park

*Posted on September 9, 2015*

As I left Fairbanks on Highway 3 south I kept seeing this monster of a mountain in the distance. I thought could it be – am I seeing Mt. McKinley from here!

I pulled over to take a picture as I was not sure if the clouds would move in by the time I got to Denali National Park (which turns out was a good move)!

At just 120 miles south of Fairbanks it was a wonderful trip to take on the way to Anchorage or if you have the time to spend a few days to do hiking / fishing! Trails are maintained and you can even take a ranger led hike if preferred!

During the day I was there hiking in the main area was restricted to the road as the moose were "rutting" and so for pictures you could not leave the roadway either. Although through my 15 mile road trip into the park I did not have the luck for moose viewing. I did get a very distant viewing (through a neighbors binoculars) of 3 mountain sheep just hanging out way up high.

Since my morning departure the clouds had also moved into the area and Mt. McKinley was just a dark outline behind the thick clouds. So glad that I was able to view its greatness from such a distance earlier that morning.

Alaska is not called the final frontier for nothing and the magnificence of the valley you drive into for Denali is breathtakingly huge! You are so very small as the millions of years old mountains look down on you – as if to say – "welcome, enjoy". Take a deep breath and just enjoy the magnificence that is Alaska as she gives you so many gifts each day if you are open to receiving them – and Denali is one of many!

See more photos of my day in Denali on my photo-share site: https://bt2bt.smugmug.com/Denali-NP-Alaska

# The Final Frontier

*Posted on September 10, 2015*

"Hey world what do you say" great lyrics played as I recapped my time in Alaska!

I could not have asked for a better 4 days in Alaska! I had a little rain on day one when crossing the border then 3 days of dry bliss!

Fall was encroaching, creating a visual explosion of color! An experience I thought I had missed out on in the eastern states as I was too early for the changing of the leaves but oh did I catch it in Alaska. Beautiful yellows floated down softly as the leaves of Aspen trees fell – what a gift to ride through. There were bushes of bright red and even the contrast of dead trees and green trees sparked ocular bliss...could not complain at all for my time in Alaska.

Not to mention the Dalton Highway. I had seen pictures
from just the week before and the rough muddy path – I
wanted to make the Arctic Circle – Amelia and I!

First step – I stopped at the gas station bought an extra
back up gas canister – topped off, adjusted chain and we
were off! The road changed probably 5 times from
gravel, packed dirt, 1/2 paved and gravel, paved, and a
muddy mess a one point! I tried to photograph the
changes in the road with my Sena 10c helmet camera To
show the challenges and extreme fun Amelia and I had
on the Dalton Highway! And I am happy to report we
made it! And we even had a little side trip to view up
close part of the Alaskan Pipeline.

My entire ride back west and north everyone I
encountered found it necessary to tell me that I was late
in the season to be heading to Alaska (as if I was not
aware of the time of year) but in all actuality I was
behind about 3 weeks for a decision made to fly to and
ride Cambodia with the Ride of My Life crew...and I
would make the same choice again.

What it meant is that I was riding faster and longer that
is all...I still saw all that I hoped too and did all that I
wanted to accomplish... and the universe in the true
nature of this trip- made sure I was here exactly when I
was supposed to be. If I reached Canada 2.5 weeks
before it was snowing in Calgary and hailing in Banff
instead when I went through (yes there was rain almost
the entire time) but the weather was so nice that I was
even able to camp through the national parks! And lets
talk Alaska if I had been just 3 days earlier they were
under a winter storm warning and the day after I
arrived (the Dalton Hwy Day) it was clear and in 60
degrees – it was perfect! I had this temperature for 3
days and was able to camp on eagle creek river near

Anchorage with the low only in the 50's. My timing –
turns out- was exactly the right time I was supposed to
be here and what can be said about hitting the 49th and
final state in my 50 state tour that can be driven to! It
was wonderful and completely filled with passion and
excitement and I found myself often just giving Amelia a
pat and smiling while exhaling a calm "Man, Alaska –
eh!"

Wildlife wise I was able to see Moose 2 separate
occasions, the second time I could see something far
ahead crossing the road – I could see the stride and the
darkness from such a distance! These creatures are
huge and utterly captivating. I sat on the side of the road
and watched a young one for quite a bit as he / she
scampered in the field of trees and bushes on the side of
the road.

See more pictures from my time in Alaska and weeks of
Galleries from my trip on my photo-share site:

http://www.BT2BT.smugmug.com

# To SHIP or not to SHIP

*Posted on September 11, 2015*

That was the question. I went back and forth and weeks
of research on shipping my Amelia to Hawaii. I looked
into planes and boats, and then also had to add weather
into the picture as has been the case on much of this
journey.

I could ship Amelia from Alaska for about $2200 and it
would take over 2 weeks to a month for her to arrive in
Hawaii or I could ride back to Southern California and
ship from San Deigo for approx. $900 and 3 day wait.
Both would be crated and ready to ships across the
ocean. The same ocean that in the last 2 weeks has had
3 category 5 hurricanes in the path to Hawaii. ( You may
have heard about the national weather service flash
flood warnings that have occurred often lately here in
HI- and seen the pictures of the sewage overflow into
the beaches because of this.)

So I made the decision that was right for me – with just 4 full days in Hawaii I would not risk the loss of shipping or being stuck without Amelia and having to rent anyways.

Today riding Hawaii – day 2 of riding I got caught in a storm but thanks to my Sena 10c that gets radio I was able to have the weather warning of exactly where the flash flooding was and I routed around it. I got soaked with the rain but made it safely around the storms. And as I sit writing this another severe weather and flash flood warning are coming in for the next 3 hours.

My Guinness World Record has to be on the same bike – it is for Longest Journey in Single Country on Motorcycle – Guinness will only count my miles in the lower 48 but to hold that record title "in single country" call me a purist – I wanted to really ride the country-all 50 states.

It was important to me that I rode a Bonneville here in Hawaii -not just any bike. So I rented a Limited Edition T-100 – the 110 year Anniversary Model as a celebratory ride and anniversary of my own. There were only 1000 of these bikes made in 2012 and I rode number 510! Hitting Hawaii means I made my trip goal – I created and began planning this trip almost 3 years ago and to hit number 50 is very exciting. All 50 states and Canada on a Bonneville in a year! But I am not done yet.

From here I will fly back to Alaska – uncover Amelia's chilly bones and hop on a ferry through the inner passages of Alaska. I will land in Bellingham, WA back on the mainland on my 1 year anniversary Sept 19th. I will then spend time with my brothers in Washington to celebrate this journey and fantastic undertaking and finally head south home to visit friends and family in Arizona near the end of September! I will of course still be traveling as I head home and there are still sites to see that I have not explored.

Although sad to have not had Amelia in Hawaii it was a beautiful ride throughout the island of Oahu. Many sites to see and even enjoyed the perfect campsite right on the ocean of the north shores- my own little private beach! During my sunset swim I was joined by 2 sea turtles – it was quite magical.

I look forward to the next and last few weeks of this journey and seeing what it all will hold. After I arrive home I will submit for the GWR and hopefully have news soon that I am new record holder!!

# Amelia and Santa's Sleigh

*Posted on September 12, 2015*

A short story – ( this is a fun work of fiction inspired by a visit to the North Pole Alaska during my year long journey with my motorcycle – a Triumph Bonneville named Amelia – just a funny little "doodle" of words.)

"It is Santa," she exclaimed with excitement! Is my headlight bright enough to lead Santa's sleigh she wondered. There it was just sitting in the field empty and no one else around. So she down shifted into 2nd rolled out on the gravel road and lined up to deliver happiness to children all around the world.

Then she wondered, "but what happiness could I bring, the sleigh was empty, no presents to give." She turned her key off and pondered this point for a moment deciding to leave the "house of Santa" and take back where she felt most at home – the open road.

"But what do I have to give if there are no presents..."
then she saw a young girl who also called this open road
home...Amelia and the young girl met and would have
many adventures together. It turns out that the present
Amelia had all along – was that she was Amelia! That
was all that was needed – a Bonneville and the open
road – Happy Christmas in September!

# *"Ponderance"

Posted on September 20, 2015

A few weeks ago I began pondering with the vastness of Alaska vanishing below me as I flew to Hawaii. I could not believe I was almost finishing my year on the road. It has been so much....well so much more than I ever thought and filling for my heart and soul and allowing a growth in areas I did not even know could expand.

I have been challenged in ways that I did not know before and stretched in ways that have made me a better and stronger person. I have become more raw to the connections and the importance of them between people, and the raw emotion that started around month 4 is still ever-present.

The wonderful thing about a journey of this magnitude is that you will carry it with you for the rest of your life, and doubly beautiful is that hopefully it is just one of many!

So on a bike that is a "street bike" I put on over 53,000 miles and covered ground in all 50 states and 3 provinces of Canada! (completed over 40,000 miles toward a Guinness World Record ride in the lower 48 states-will go into application process as soon as I return home in late – Sept.) Amelia did amazing and only needed routine maintenance, it is odd how your bike becomes a bit of a companion as you venture alone out there – sometimes on quite deserted roads. I was very proud of many of the roads we took on together – the Blue Ridge Parkway, Tail of the Dragon, the Dalton Highway, Natchez Trace, the Arctic Circle, and so much more!

I have camped in every state and seen family in many states that I have not seen in years, and friends that were long distance are now rekindled connections! I don't think I can fully process this journey (first because it is not over – I still have a good 1500 miles to ride) but just the enormity of the journey – it will be wonderful to go back and read my journals and create the chapters for the book that will be written from this adventure! It will be in this process that memories fly back into clear view and I will be able to see as I look back how they changed me...I feel calmer and a little more distant which is something that I am sure will make acclimation back into "life" ( I don't say real or normal life because I believe my real life – non-normal: is ingrained and will not change)... a little different and a challenge in itself.

Only time will tell how the reintegration goes but for now I still have over a week of riding to complete and more new sites to see along the winding path home!

*"ponderance" before I get critics saying – weird that is not a word...I like the composition of it so I am taking artistic / poetic license as it fits for this entry – and

depending on how you define it, or look up its meaning, it makes it into some forms of the dictionary.

# Home ???

*Posted on September 22, 2015*

Are you ever coming home?

I have a small handful of very good friends back in Arizona and from one of them in Phoenix -on a happy birthday text- she wrote -"Happy Birthday, miss you – are you ever coming home?"

This was such a perfect statement to the freedom and excitement the open roads holds. There are things that we can change about ourselves (and thank god for that – because we all need a little maintenance every now and then) but for the parts that are almost ingrained...these are hard to lose and get rid of...and I would never try.

The wildness within a heart to just be open in the world is such a luxury in this day and age because it is possible to see the world in ways that other generations did not have open to them. And the fact that my friend knows my heart so well...and honestly if I had funding or found a way to create the funds to be on the road or a citizen of the world changing home every few months...I probably would (I am always looking at new possibilities) which is why this made me laugh and cry!

Laugh because it is so true to my being – "are you ever coming home" and cry because – I never have felt at home anywhere – I grew up moving a lot but being gone and having very close friends in AZ and much of my family- is Arizona home?  I wondered! I really don't like the summer heat but I also have never had friends like those I have right now and maybe right now Arizona will be home! And when it is time to change then it will change again. For now after this journey I am returning to Arizona – for how long – it is too soon to tell as there are a few exciting options on the table and maybe I will be back on the open road in just 7- 9 months – only time will tell.

DANELL LYNN

## October 2015

### GWR a Journey in Itself
*October 26, 2015 // 11 Comments*

Today is a big day, and one that feels so good to have under my belt. I had quite the ordeal getting all the paperwork in order and the proper files downloaded (not user [...]

### What Inspired This
*October 12, 2015 // 2 Comments*

People often ask what inspired me to take this trip and I never had a clear and short answer...I guess the simplest I could make is to answer – LIFE! If you have [...]

### Amelia's Officially Amazing
*March 12, 2016 // 10 Comments*

It has been many hours of tracking and applications, and more spent riding and enjoying this vast world we are all lucky to share! It is official – Amelia and I have [...]

# What Inspired This

*Posted on October 12, 2015*

People often ask what inspired me to take this trip and I never had a clear and short answer...I guess the simplest I could make is to answer – LIFE!

If you have caught my talk on the journey and the inspirational 4 min video I created I cover different things from childhood to adulthood that helped to shape the person I am- which is the person who made the choice to take on such a journey.

While on the journey inspiration can change and occasionally being moved by those that you may be inspiring. It is this young girl – in the image below that makes me want to write better, tell stories more, travel more and inspire those that are not sure they want to get out there...or to those young and wild souls like

Zoe's. And to the parents of these "different" and "independent" hearts – cheers to you as we are not the easiest to raise! But to all the parents out there that open little hearts to the world through literature or experiential travel much love your way. And a big high-five to those like little Zoe's family that have your "little girls" on bikes!

I have been communicating with her family as I have traveled and she is one of my biggest supporters and has big dreams of travel and motorcycles. I have this picture saved on my I-pad and until this blog maybe she did not know that she is also my inspiration – If having a rough day out there on the road, I just looked at that photo and it brought a big smile to my face and reminded me how great this journey is and the journey of life! So to Zoe – thank you!

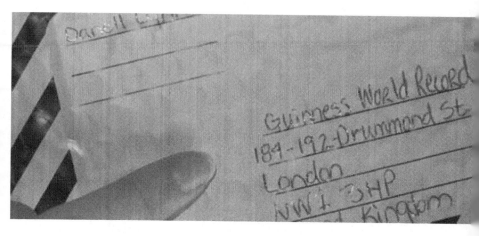

# GWR a Journey in Itself

*Posted on October 26, 2015*

Today is a big day, and one that feels so good to have under my belt. I had quite the ordeal getting all the paperwork in order and the proper files downloaded (not user error it was a site error from my satellite tracker) but alas...after many hours and much additional evidence scanned in...I am proud to say the package is in the mail! She is complete and London bound to the Guinness World Record headquarters!

Although there was much to track it was fun to see all the elements of the journey and create 214 photo spread of evidence and catalog the videos and even the receipts input – that will be nice to have organized when I start writing the official book!

Cheers to everyone who has followed this journey and now that Guinness is submitted I will get back to giving you more write ups from the year on the road and more episodes starting with the Episode 8:

https://youtu.be/i7Oqv9W_iF0

https://youtu.be/7g7DbH4hGgw

https://youtu.be/0uhPYja5ZYc

https://youtu.be/wzeXF2TUHGA

https://youtu.be/Jq9ySKM5gjM

ALLY **AMAZING** **Longest journey by motorcyc single country**

The longest journey by motorcycle in a single country is 78,214,118 km (48,600 miles) and was achieved by Danell Lynn (USA), who rode throughout the United States of America from 19 September 2014 to 29 August 2015.

During this journey, Danell rode through all 48 of the continental United States.

Who
**DANELL L'**

What
**78214.118**

Where
**UNITED ST**
PHOENIX

# Amelia's Officially Amazing

*Posted on March 12, 2016*

It has been many hours of tracking and applications, and more spent riding and enjoying this vast world we are all lucky to share!

It is official – Amelia and I have broken the Guinness World Record, Longest Journey in a Single Country by Motorcycle, breaking the previous record by more than 20,000 miles!! Honored, excited,...for a blog and a post – words evade me! Thanks for staying on the journey with me! Hell of a ride for sure.

The GWR is only calculated for the lower 48 states, as I crossed into Canada for Alaska and flew to Hawaii – so although my entire journey was over 53,000 miles in a year, and all 50 states – the GWR was calculated by my time in the continental United States for the record break!

Thank you for coming on the journey with me. The blog www.BlackTie2BlackTop.com is still active under www.DanellLynn.wordpress.com and catalogs all the journeys I am still taking.

For more visit www.DanellLynn.com and I hope to see you out there on the road! Cheers and ride safe.

This journey has led to more opportunities to speak including AMA Vintage Days, Keynote for Mountain Moxie and Mid-Atlantic Women's Motorcycle Rally, countless dealerships, many schools and university and hopefully many more to come. if you are interested in booking a motivational lecture or how to...visit www.danelllynn.com/speaking.

And not to be forgotten – THE FUNDING–

Okay let be clear – I had no financial sponsorship – people often say, "oh you could do it because you were sponsored!" I did have gear and kit sponsors – but nothing that I did not already have – just a lot better quality of gear and kit, I would have still departed- I am very thankful to REV'IT for my gear, GiantLoop for my luggage, LoneRider for my home away from home – tent, British Customs for my gel seat and pips, and after month 7 on the road I excitedly received AVON tires and parts provided by Triumph North America. My sponsors were amazing and the product they provided gave me a wonderful ride – but let's get back to the money part!

When I was preparing for this road trip I did this really weird thing, this old school thing…I saved for 2 years! My goal was $25,000 but I did not reach it – I had a departure date and no matter what I had I would make it work. So on September 19th, 2014 I departed for a year long journey (ended up 374 days) and I spent approximately $18,500. Now if you need to hotel every night your budget would be different – but I had an amazing trip and would not change it!

DANELL LYNN

# ABOUT THE AUTHOR

Danell Lynn an adventurer and Guinness World Record globe trotter. She is the first solo-woman ever to break the world record for Longest Journey by Motorcycle in a Single country (BlackTie2BlackTop). She currently holds that record with 48,600 miles. Danell was the sole female rider in The Ride of My Life - Cambodia Documentary, and for Expedition Electric. She continues to do humanitarian work throughout the globe with her foundations Threading Hope and Highwire.

She has traveled to more than 45 countries and has a life goal of keeping the number of countries visited larger than the number of her years on this earth, and believes in a life fully lived!

She is the author of *Philanthropic Wanderlust, Purposeful Wanderings,* and a Cultural Coloring book series for children. She was the founding editor of *2 Wheeled Wanderlust the Magazine* and was a contributing columnist for *Mainstream Magazine* – Philanthropy-Mainstream Cares, previous Lifestyle Editor and Destination Columnist for *Phoenix SportBike Magazine,* and Arts Editor for *The Noise Newspaper.*

She is the designer and owner of dl-couture a custom high fashion line which has dressed Mrs. World, Miss America, and more...She also created Humani Handbags an elegant twist on fashion, function and philanthropy.

She has been a nominee for the Governors Arts Awards of-Arizona (2011 and 2014), recipient of a gratitude award by the First Lady of El Salvador, and has been featured on numerous television and radio programs. (Good Morning AZ, FOX 10 Sports News, Adventure Rider Radio,FOX 10 AZ-AM, KNAU- NPR Radio, NPR-Weekend Edition,...) and in many magazines and newspaper nationally and internationally (AMA -cover story, Overland Magazine, ADV Moto, So Scottsdale, Motorcycle Explorer, Uptown magazine, Outdoorx4, AZ Daily Sun,...)

48792853R00139

Made in the USA
San Bernardino, CA
04 May 2017